BLOCK PRINTS

How To Make Them

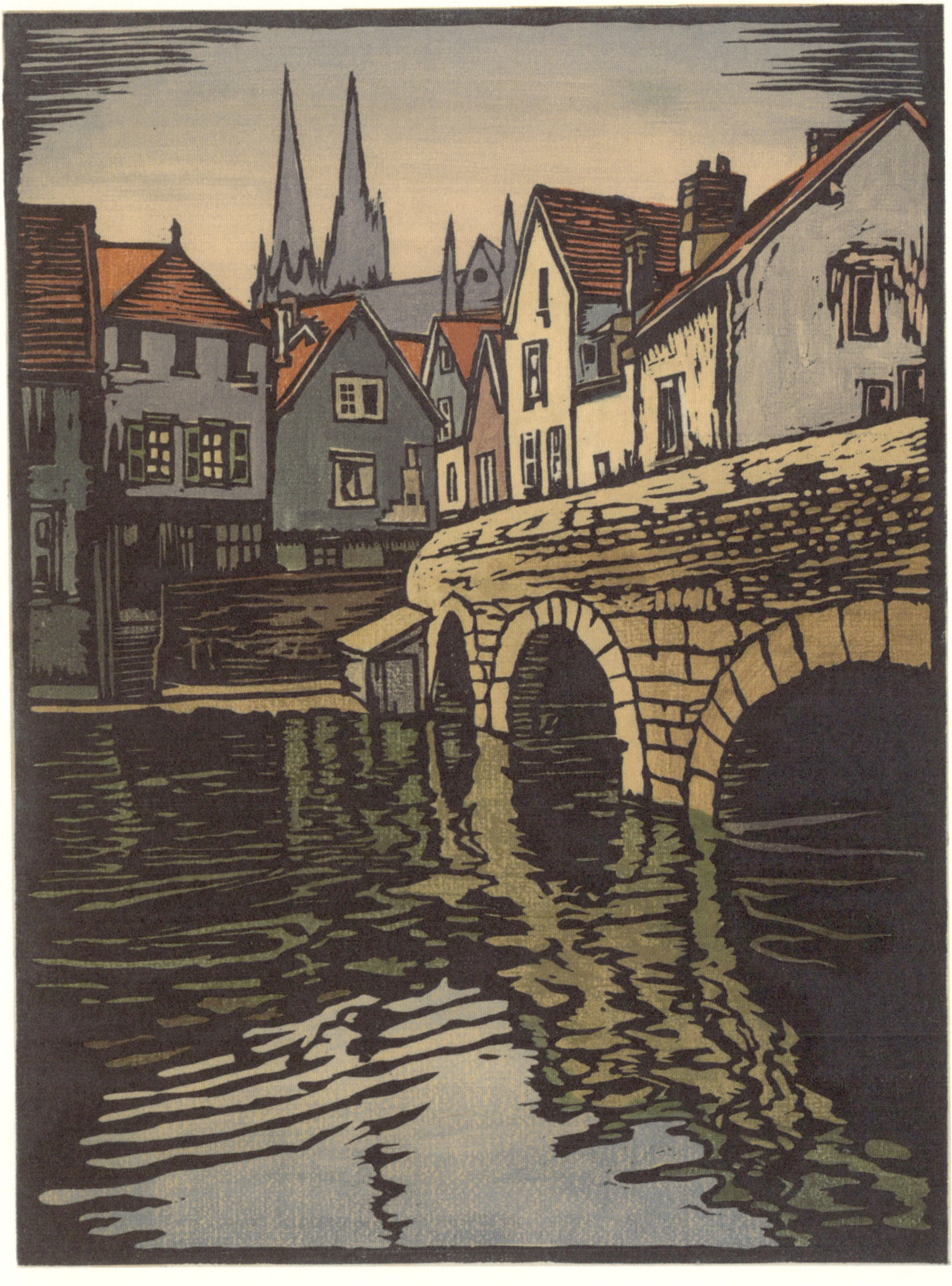

Old Bridge—Chartres
From a color block print by William S. Rice

BLOCK PRINTS

How To Make Them

WILLIAM S. RICE

Second Edition

Introduction and Notes by

Martin Krause

Pomegranate

PORTLAND, OREGON

Pomegranate Communications, Inc.
105 SE 18th Ave., Portland, OR 97214
800-227-1428 pomegranate.com
sales@pomegranate.com

To learn about our newest titles and special offers from Pomegranate, please visit pomegranate.com and sign up for our newsletter. For all other queries, see "Contact Us" on our home page.

First edition published 1941. Second edition 2019.

A note to the modern edition:
This book is unabridged and faithful to the original publication. It is not identical, however, and a few differences can be noted: Two pages, listing reference books and sources for block printing supplies, useful in 1941, have been omitted. Where necessary for readability, minor changes have been made in punctuation and syntax. Occasional layout changes have resulted from the inclusion of Martin Krause's modern introduction and annotations.

Front cover: *Barn in Calaveras*
Back cover: *Windmill, Golden Gate Park*

Library of Congress Cataloging-in-Publication Data
Names: Rice, William S. (William Seltzer), 1873-1963, author. | Krause, Martin F., editor, writer of introduction.
Title: Block prints : how to make them / William S. Rice ; introduction by Martin Krause.
Description: Portland, Oregon : Pomegranate, 2019.
Identifiers: LCCN 2018041427 | ISBN 9780764984327 (hardcover : alk. paper)
Subjects: LCSH: Linoleum block-printing--Technique.
Classification: LCC NE1330 .R48 2019 | DDC 761/.3--dc23
LC record available at https://lccn.loc.gov/2018041427

Item No. A278
Designed by Patrice Morris

Printed in China

35 34 33 32 31 30 29 28 27 26 12 11 10 9 8 7 6 5 4 3

CONTENTS

INTRODUCTION

In his preface to *Block Prints: How To Make Them,* William S. Rice promises any serious reader useful instruction in the graphic art in which Rice specialized. His 1941 illustrated manual fully describes the design, cutting, and printing of relief prints—printed from one block or several, carved from linoleum or wood—as applied to either fine art printmaking suitable for framing or to the more utilitarian arts of lettering, holiday card production, and bookplate creation. His guide describes straightforward, step-by-step solutions to the intricate challenges of block printmaking in both advanced and home-studio settings, written with the authority of one who had tested them all. His methods rely on his forty years as an art instructor in California public schools and his twenty-five years as a national exhibitor of block prints, in color and in black and white.

Rice had a practical mind and received a practical education. When he enrolled at the Pennsylvania Museum and School of Industrial Art in Philadelphia in 1892, its circular assured each future graduate that "if industrious and energetic, he is in no danger of being pushed to the wall in the struggle for existence." Having submitted the prize-winning drawing to a contest sponsored by the *Philadelphia Times* in 1895, Rice was rewarded with a position on the newspaper as a staff artist. Rice then studied pen-and-ink drawing and illustration at Drexel Institute of Art, Science, and Industry under the influential Howard Pyle in pursuit of a career as an illustrator. In 1900, a former classmate, Frederick Meyer, lured him west with an offer to teach drawing in the Stockton, California, public schools.

Early in his California years, Rice developed a penchant for submitting freelance articles to periodicals and illustrating them with either his photo-engraved line drawings or his artistic photographs. He shared his close observations of nature in descriptions of rambles from the High Sierra to the deserts of New Mexico and supplemented his teacher's salary in the process. Other submissions outlined his pedagogical methods in such publications as the *School Arts Book,* later known as the *School Arts Magazine.* He thus embarked on a second career as a regular provider of clear, thoughtful, applicable advice on the variety of art skills that he was professionally mastering as part of the art curriculum while in Stockton. This continued through subsequent professional moves to secondary schools in Alameda, in 1910, and in Oakland, in 1914, from which he retired in 1940.

Rice's interest in printmaking dates to his move to the East Bay in 1910. He began teaching drawing and watercolor painting in the summers at the California School of Arts and Crafts, organized by his friend Meyer in the old Commercial High School building in Berkeley, where the noted etcher Perham Nahl also taught. Three of Rice's early etchings were displayed at the *Third Annual Exhibition of the California Society of Etchers* in San Francisco in 1914, two of which depended on sketches Rice made on his sketching tour to Europe the previous summer. His new passion for block printing coincided with the surprising impact of color woodblock prints within the vast array of art displayed in the Palace of Fine Arts at San Francisco's Panama-Pacific International Exposition in 1915. Etching had always been the unassailable king of juried exhibitions, but for the first time, a fair share of the awards in the graphic arts division went to American block printmakers, including a gold medal to Gustave Baumann, an unknown from Nashville, Indiana. Furthermore, Japanese galleries were enlivened by the many small color woodblock prints of the sort that had caused a sensation in the art world when first encountered by the West forty years earlier. For Rice, the exposition was a continuous revelation as he and his new bride frequently crossed the bay during the nine months of the exposition. According to their daughter Roberta Rice Treseder, "The World's Fair was, of course, a big event for [my parents], too. For Will, it was a turning point in his appreciation of Japanese woodcuts and prints." Rice became a collector, a practitioner of the Japanese printing method, and an emulator of the aesthetics of Ando Hiroshige and Katsushika Hokusai, to whose delightful woodcut landscapes he had been introduced.

For an artist who had already mastered and taught such useful Arts and Crafts staples as leather tooling, coppersmithing, and applied design, an interest in block printmaking—a quintessential art and craft—would be natural. He may well have dabbled in it years earlier, but his first documented color block print is a 1915 Christmas card.

Rice could indulge his new enthusiasm at home. Basic tools, wood or linoleum blocks, inks, and papers were all that were needed for tabletop printing, unlike the expensive and sophisticated materials needed to etch. He may have been guided by his copy of F. Morley Fletcher's 1916 *Wood-Block Printing: A Description of the Craft of Woodcutting and Colourprinting Based on the Japanese Practice*. He had five block prints of Scottish and Bay Area subjects ready for the *Sixth Annual Exhibition of the California Society of Etchers* in the spring of 1917, and that fall he mounted a small solo showing of his new prints at the Oakland Municipal Art Gallery, described in the *Oakland Tribune* on October 28 as "colorful, strong, and imaginative." He gave an accompanying talk on block-printing techniques and referred to the European, American, and Japanese masters whose work he had encountered on the walls of the fair. He singled out Baumann. He praised Arthur Wesley Dow, the dean of American block printmakers and the author of *Composition: Understanding Line, Notan and Color,* a book on the nature of visual representation drawn from Japanese traditions that was enormously influential on art instructors in turn-of-the-century America, including Rice. He admired Bertha Lum's pictures of Japanese life, crafted and printed by traditional methods in Japan. He also cited the work of Bay Area printmaker Pedro J. Lemos, with whom Rice had already struck up an association and friendship that would be lifelong. Echoing his own experimental proclivities, Rice quoted from Dow's 1916 article in the *International Studio,* "Printing from Wood Blocks," noting that block printing "is a painter's art, for creative colour is the aim and purpose of the whole thing. It is a free craft, for the artist is his own engraver, printer, and publisher, producing, by hand, single prints, no two alike." This first show was superseded in 1918 by a major solo exhibition of about thirty block prints sponsored by the San Francisco Art Association at the Palace of Fine Arts. With Rice's inclusion in the seminal 1919 *Wood Block Prints in Color by American Artists* at the Detroit Institute of Arts, he had rapidly become an artist of national renown.

Rice worked in an attic studio at the top of his Craftsman bungalow on Rosedale Avenue in East Oakland, which was vividly described in the *Oakland Tribune* on January 4, 1925: "There is no sign of Bohemia here; no stale and dying cigarettes, no litter of ashes, no couches, no pillows, no place to loaf. For Rice's studio is a work room, where real work is going on, splendid, vigorous work." His studio would come to have a professional handpress for printing very large blocks, but it was also equipped with a homemade, portable, wooden "printing frame" and a handy clothes wringer, both functioning as basic presses, which Rice used in the classroom and when experimenting at home. Blocks could be aligned in the printing frame, inked, overlaid with a sheet of Japanese paper, and rubbed with a disc-like burnishing tool known as a baren to transfer the design. The wringer could print thin unmounted blocks of linoleum run between the two superimposed hard rollers. Rice's experiences as a printmaker of both simple and complicated images created by both elemental and complex means, coupled with his amalgamated skills as an artist, educator, designer, and writer, coalesced in the condensed, eminently readable, and useful guide *Block Prints: How To Make Them,* Rice's most popular and widely read art manual.

Martin Krause, Curator Emeritus
Indianapolis Museum of Art at Newfields

PREFACE TO THE FIRST EDITION

This book was prepared in response to numerous requests for practical instruction in the art of block printing from students in art schools and teachers in public schools and teachers' colleges. It is offered with the sincere hope that it may prove both instructive and encouraging to those who are seriously interested in this most absorbing handicraft.

As a school problem, block printing is full of interest and has many applications. It stimulates the creative faculty, yet, because of the limitations of the medium, it restricts and controls the imagination.

Interest in block printing is growing in the schools and colleges from year to year, as indicated by the well executed block-print illustrations found in their periodicals, posters, and announcements.

Acknowledgment is gratefully made to my students of the California College of Arts and Crafts, Oakland, of the University of California Extension Division, Berkeley, of the Art Department of Castlemont High School, Oakland, and to fellow craftsmen who have generously allowed the author to use their linoleum cuts as illustrations in this book. All illustrations save those with a credit line are by the author.

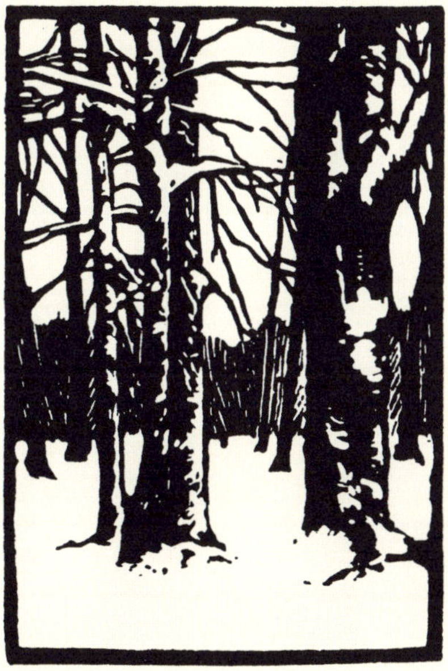

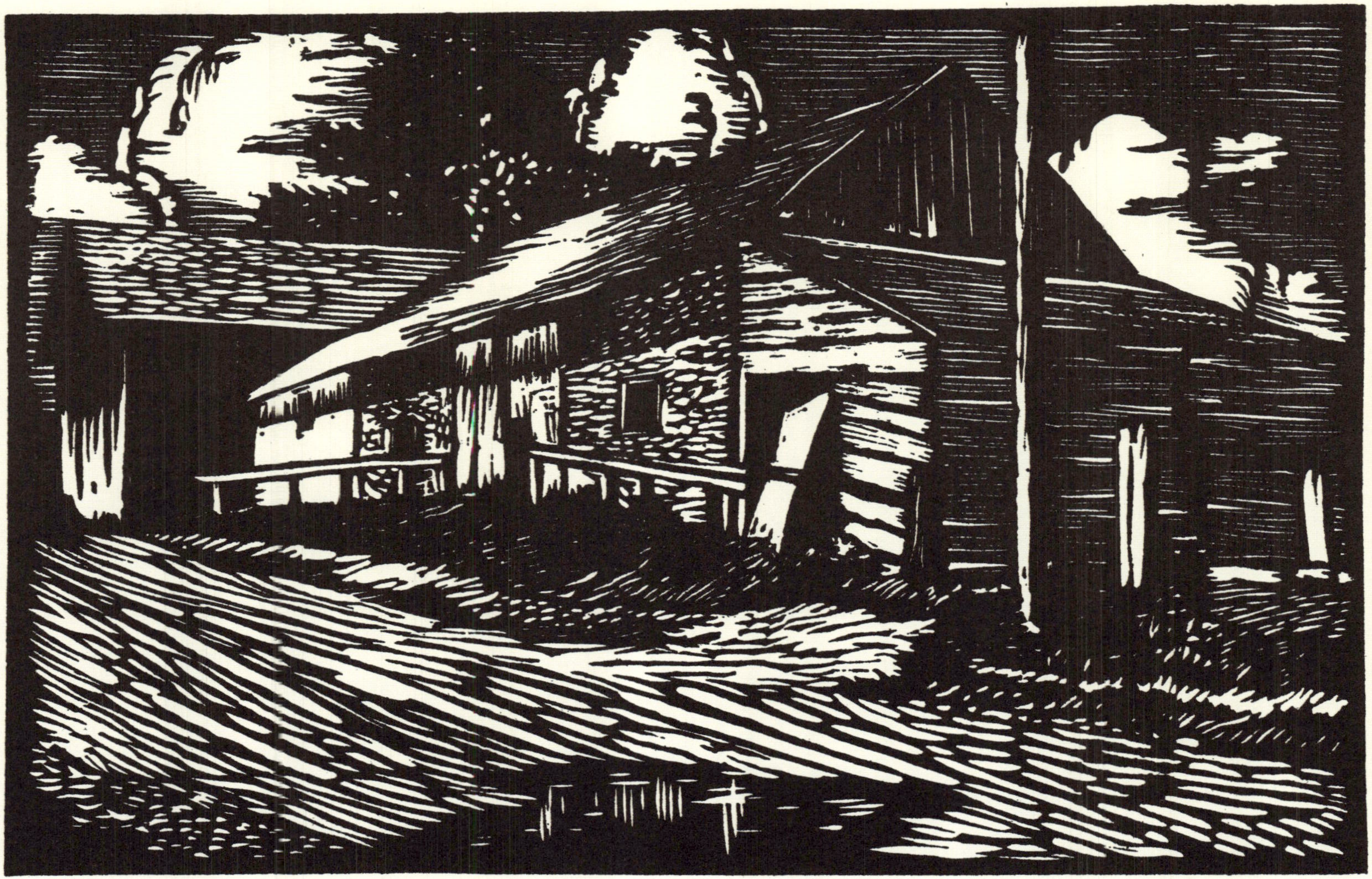

A Stone Barn—Pennsylvania

CHAPTER I

BRIEF HISTORY OF BLOCK PRINTING

The origin of block printing seems "lost in the mists of antiquity," and while its practice by the ancients is of great interest to the historian and the print collector, most students are more concerned with its technique and the methods of contemporary artists, either in the United States or abroad.

It may, however, interest students to know in a general way how this art originated and by whom it was practiced in the past. The art was employed, in a crude way, by the Egyptians several thousand years before Christ.[1] The Chinese also practiced it several centuries before the Christian era, in fact, as soon as paper was invented.[2]

From China the art of woodblock printing spread into Korea and Japan during the eighth century. The advent of this art into these neighboring countries resulted, by a gradual process of evolution, in an improvement over Chinese printing. The woodcut is the national mode of engraving in Japan, where it has been carried to a pitch of marvelous perfection.

A desire for the pleasures of art had sprung up there among the lower classes. Paintings were too expensive. Moronobu saw the enormous possibilities of the woodcut, and adapting his style to the limitations and possibilities of this medium, devoted his time to supplying the need of the people.[3]

Soon came a desire for color. Moronobu and his pupils produced broadsheets and books which were often colored by hand, tan or red lead being the dominant color.

The theater later furnished subjects for prints demanded by the populace. Torii Kiyomoto founded a famous dynasty of artists. His son, Kiyonobu, was the first to design portraits of actors – a staple theme of the print designers.[4]

In 1740 or 1741 the two-color print in rose-red and green was first published in Japan.[5] Cherrywood was used, being cut on the plank with a knife, as in Europe till the days of Bewick.[6] A separate block was cut for each color. An accurate register was obtained by means of a guide mark, in the form of a right angle at the lower corner of the key block and a straight line parallel to the lower edge at the left corner. No press was used. Instead, the paper was laid on the inked block and rubbed on the back with a baren – a pad made of cardboard covered with bamboo leaves.

Hokusai was a master of landscape. His thirty-six views of Fuji and other sets contain some of the finest landscapes ever made. A little later appeared Hiroshige, who turned out countless sets of prints depicting every aspect of his own country in every weather – rain and shine – with extraordinary intimacy and freshness.[7]

The use of cheap pigments (aniline) and lack of masters caused the art of block printing to decline in Japan.[8] However, a new style of color printing began in 1889, when the *Kokka* began to reproduce old paintings.[9] At the present time there are some remarkably beautiful and colorful prints being made which, in the author's opinion, are as fine as those produced in the past.

The process of block printing was introduced into Europe from East Asia about 1423.[10] In Germany, Dürer carried this art to a marvelous perfection. Dürer and Holbein used a black line in printing which resembled, somewhat, a pen drawing.[11] They produced illustrations of naïve religious subjects and did their work in a most accurate and painstaking way with engraving-like effects of delicacy and richness.

In eighteenth-century England, Thomas Bewick started a revolt against this traditional black-line system and developed what is known as the white-line system, whereby the design is engraved against a black background as the medium logically implies. Timothy Cole, Henry Wolf, and their contemporaries, who composed our American school of wood engravers and who worked in the 1890s before the invention of photo reproduction, carried the white-line method to its greatest perfection.[12]

Cole and Wolf were the two outstanding masters of this period; and they had the remarkable faculty of reproducing in their medium, all the delicate tonal effects of the oil paintings from which they worked. Their function was to translate a painting or photograph into a line medium that could be reproduced on the printed page.

This style of engraving flourished before the invention of the photoengraving process which revolutionized the older, less rapid, and obviously more expensive method of engraving. Naturally enough, wood engraving was then looked upon as a reproductive art rather than a medium for creative expression. The engraver was merely an expert technician or craftsman who reproduced the work of others, as painters and photographers, in a line medium that could be used in a printing press. These engravings were commonly called "woodcuts."

This traditional term "cut" is still in use among photoengravers today, although a photomechanical process is used to make them. The photoengraving process is divided into two principal divisions – the zinc or line cut, and the copper or halftone cut.[13] No description will be made here of these two forms of engravings, because the difference between them is quite obvious. We are mainly concerned with hand-cut blocks.

To the late Arthur Wesley Dow of Columbia University, we are indebted for the revival of color block printing in America.[14] Professor Dow was attracted by this medium and went to Japan to study the native methods. In 1895 he first exhibited his prints in the Boston Museum. This was one of the first attempts at color printing in this country. At that time the art had few followers and only in the last twenty years has it been taken up seriously by any great number of artists. The development was retarded, because the public was slow to appreciate this type of artwork. It is gratifying to printmakers now to know that the public is becoming interested in block prints, and that more and more, they find a ready market, especially for prints in color.

NOTES

1 Signature seals, individualized carved designs in stone (intaglios) designed for impressing in clay, were known in ancient Mesopotamia and Egypt by the beginning of the third millennium BCE.

2 The first emperor of China, Qin Shi Huang, had a signature seal carved from white jade in 221 BCE. Paper, made from rags and plant fibers, was reputedly invented in China around 105 CE by Cai Lun, a Han dynasty court official. Woodblock printmaking appeared at the beginning of the Tang dynasty (618–907 CE) and by its end was in wide use for the dissemination of knowledge and literacy. Block printed religious texts followed Buddhism from China to Korea and Japan, where independent texts were being printed by the middle of the eighth century.

3 Hishikawa Moronobu (1618–1694) was a Japanese painter-printmaker and the first master of the *ukiyo-e* ("images of the floating world") genre of Japanese art, which emphasized the sensual pleasures of urban life invogorating the peace and tranquility of the Edo period (1603–1868).

4 Torii Kiyomoto (1645–1702) was a kabuki actor and painter of kabuki theater billboards and advertisements. He was followed by his son Shobei (1664–1729), who took the name Torii Kiyonobu. This son created block-printed books depicting kabuki plays and established the genre of dynamic portraits of kabuki actors painted on signboards or printed on single sheets.

5 The exact origin of the earliest form of Japanese color woodblock printmaking, the two-block woodcut printed in red and green known as *benizuri-e* ("crimson printed pictures"), is unknown, but the method was most common from 1745 to 1755.

6 Thomas Bewick (1753–1828) was an English engraver. He is credited with the popularization of "wood engraving," carved into the hard end-grain of wood, which was more durable than the plank side typically used for woodcuts. Wood engraving allowed for the finer details needed for Bewick's illustrations of detailed flora and fauna.

7 Katsushika Hokusai (1760–1849) and Ando Hiroshige (1797–1858) were the supreme designers of landscape prints at the end of the Edo period. Their color woodcuts were avidly collected by European and American artists after the forced opening of the ports of Japan in 1854 revealed their existence to the West. Rice became personally acquainted with their work in the retrospective section of the Japanese art galleries at the 1915 Panama-Pacific International Exposition in San Francisco.

8 The first aniline dyes were synthesized in an English laboratory in 1856 and were in use in Japanese prints the following decade. They were colorfast and cheaper to produce than natural dyes, but Western collectors, like Rice, found the artificial colors harsh and gaudy.

9 The *Kokka* ("Flower of the Nation"), Japan's first art journal, began publication in 1889 to counter Japan's fascination with Western art and culture. Until 1946, most monthly issues contained an original color woodblock print, and its other color reproductions were considered among the finest anywhere.

10 The earliest-known dated European woodcut is a devotional image of St. Christopher from 1423, but undated woodcuts are likely to predate it by a decade or more.

11 Albrecht Dürer (1471–1528) and Hans Holbein the Younger (1497–1543) were two of the first masters of woodblock printmaking in Renaissance Europe. The superiority and finesse of the carvings that bear their names are due in part to the expertise of the *formschneider* (block cutter) each employed, much like Hiroshige and Hokusai turned over their designs to master cutters and printers.

12 Timothy Cole (1852–1931) and Henry Wolf (1852–1916) were American wood engravers who achieved the ultimate technical mastery of the medium. These two virtuosos specialized in engraved facsimiles of old master and contemporary paintings commissioned at the end of the nineteenth century by high-tone publications such as *Scribner's Magazine*, *Scribner's Monthly*, and the *Century*. Improvements in photoreproduction made wood engraving obsolete during their lifetimes, but both were honored with large displays at the Panama-Pacific International Exposition. Wolf showed 144 wood engravings and was awarded the Grand Prize in the graphics division.

13 Line cuts (drawings photoetched onto zinc printing plates) replaced wood engravings for published

NOTES *(continued)*

reproductions in the last two decades of the nineteenth century. The halftone process, a variant of line cutting allowing for the reproduction of gray-scale tones, as its name implies, was patented in 1881 and was in general use by the turn of the century.

14 Arthur Wesley Dow (1857–1922) was the dean of American color woodblock printmakers and the most influential art educator of his era. He furthered his early admiration for Japanese art under the curator for Oriental art at the Museum of Fine Arts, Boston, Ernest Fenollosa, who returned in 1890 from twelve years in Japan. Dow began creating his own color woodcuts in 1892, was hired by Fenollosa as assistant curator in 1893, and was given a solo show of his woodcuts at the museum in 1895. In 1899 Dow published *Composition*, a teaching manual that stipulated that art should be decorative as well as pictorial and built from arrangements of line, mass, and color rather than from a slavish imitation of nature. He trained an entire generation of the nation's art instructors, first at the Pratt Institute in Brooklyn and then, from 1903, at the Columbia University Teachers College in New York City.

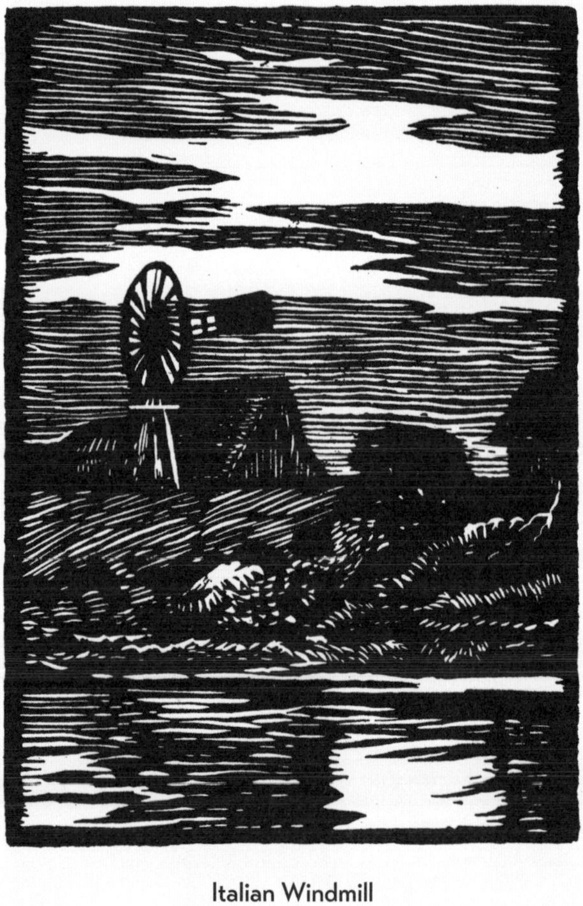

Italian Windmill

CHAPTER II

PREPARING THE DESIGN

The art of making "linocuts" or linoleum-block prints may be divided into three parts: first, the design, second, the cutting, and third, the printing; but, "lest we forget, the greatest of these is the design."

In order to make a suitable design that may be carried out in a block printing, it will be necessary to consider the limitations as well as the characteristics of the medium. Linoleum, as a medium for cutting, demands large, bold masses with luminous contrasts in black and white.[1] This material will, with time and care, respond beautifully to delicate cutting, where needed, and produce subtle effects of texture.

Subjects may be obtained by sketching in pencil direct from nature, by painting in watercolor, or by using original snapshots. Furthermore, abstract designs done in the modern manner are quite suitable for this craft.

The next step is to rule a space, the exact size of the block you wish to cut, on the thinnest kind of Japanese paper. If this cannot be obtained, ordinary white tissue may be substituted. Lay the paper on the sketch and trace it. For this you should use a No. 4 watercolor brush and waterproof India ink.[2] This tracing should look exactly like the print is to look when it is finished. There will be some slight variations in the finished print because each cutting tool leaves a characteristic mark.

Because of the limitations of the medium, the design should be kept simple with little or no detail. A silhouette is really an ideal subject for a beginner. Do not make a hasty sketch and then imagine that the design will improve in the cutting! Draw it as carefully as though it were intended for the engraver for reproduction. It must be made exactly the same size that the print is to be when finished. When the design is complete in all its details, the next step is to transfer it to the block. There are several methods of doing this.

The first and simplest method is to draw directly on the block with crayon, pencil, charcoal, or India ink. The main difficulty is that the design must be drawn in reverse on the block. Otherwise it would reverse in printing. When the design contains lettering, each letter as well as the whole design must be drawn in reverse. Linoleum blocks are easer to sketch upon, if first coated with white poster paint.

The second method, and one which has been found most practical, is to glue the tracing design facedown on the block. To insure its sticking thoroughly, spread the glue (not mucilage or library paste) evenly on the block with the fingers and scrape off the superfluous glue with a palette knife. Then lay the tracing facedown on the glued block, gently pressing it down evenly all over the surface. Care must be taken not to tear the paper in smoothing out the wrinkles.

Many of the modern linoleums have a lacquered finish. The glued design will not stick to this kind of surface, unless it is thoroughly sandpapered before pasting. Olive oil or Vaseline rubbed on the back of the design tends to make it transparent, thus making the pattern easier to follow.

Another method that some craftsmen follow is to slip carbon paper under the reversed tracing or drawing, and to tack the whole assembly to the block which has first been thinly painted with white show card color.[3] Then the entire design is gone over with a hard pencil or pointed instrument.

Textile Motif—Student

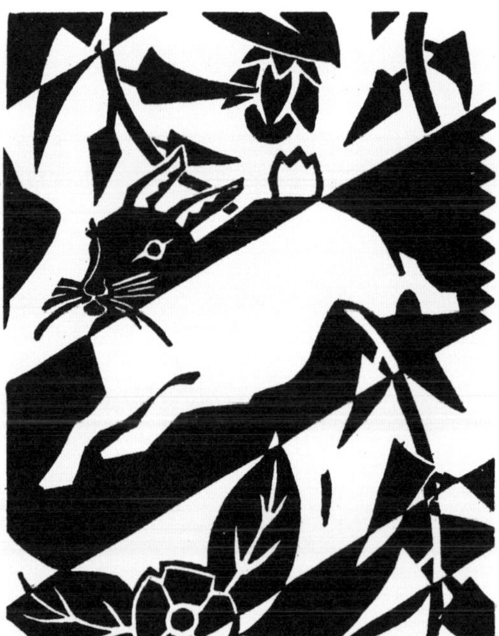

Allover Design—Student

Still another method recommended by a noted craftsman is to transfer the inked design in reverse directly on the block. The method is as follows: A drawing is made with waterproof India ink on very thin paper. Then a piece of blotting paper, somewhat larger than the drawing, is laid upon a folded newspaper. The blotter is saturated with ordinary household ammonia. The drawing, inked side up, is laid upon the wet blotter and pressed until it becomes saturated and lies flat. The linoleum block (sandpapered first) is laid facedown on the drawing and the whole thing put under a letterpress.[4] Considerable pressure is required. The time needed to make the transfer varies from one minute to fifteen or more.

There are other methods of transferring which need not be discussed.

Regardless of the method, the transferred design should be inked in on the block with drawing ink. Areas which will be cut away remain white; the other areas are filled in with ink.

LIST OF MATERIALS NEEDED FOR BLOCK PRINTING

1. Paper – Japanese tissue, Hosho paper, colored construction papers, newsprint.[5]
2. India ink for the sketch to be made on Japanese tissue paper.
3. Brush – No. 4 sable or camel hair, or Japanese brush.
4. Tube of glue to stick design to block.
5. Battleship linoleum, preferably ⅛ inch thick when mounted on type-high blocks, and ¼ inch thick when unmounted.[6]
6. Set of cutting tools (U- and V-shaped gouges).
7. Palette knife for mixing inks.
8. Kerosene for cleaning blocks.
9. Block-printing inks (black, white, and the primary colors).
10. Jar of white show card color.
11. Pane of glass with white paper pasted underneath to be used as a mixing slab or palette. A white marble slab may be substituted.
12. Brayer or ink roller to spread ink on the engraved block.
13. Stencil knife and some razor blades.
14. A thinning medium for the inks, made of common lard and magnesia. Commercially called Flattine.[7] This also takes the shine off the inks.
15. Oilstone for sharpening tools.
16. A letterpress, clothes wringer, printing frame, or etching press for the printing.[8]
17. Three pieces of cardboard 9 by 12 inch, the middle one to be cut like a "mat" and the other two to be used as covers. These are hinged together at the top with gummed tape and form a "kit" or "jig," in which to lock the block securely and prevent its skidding when the wringer or etching press is used instead of the letterpress. It is best to leave the blocks unmounted, when the wringer or etching press is used. The reason for this is that the space between the rollers is limited.
18. Several flat sable brushes to paint the colors on the blocks.
19. Plenty of rags to clean blocks and palette.
20. Fine sandpaper for cleaning rough or lacquer surfaces of linoleum.
21. Thumbtacks.
22. Burnisher – glass or metal caster cup, or cornhusk baren.
23. Inexpensive material as percale, unbleached muslin, linen, sateen, etc., for textile printing.
24. Hammer or wooden mallet to be used in printing on textiles.

NOTES

1 Linoleum, from the Latin for *flax* and *oil*, is a flexible, durable, rubbery material made of linseed (flaxseed) oil, pine rosin, and wood particles. Discovered and patented in the mid-nineteenth century, it has been employed as an alternative for wood in block printmaking since the early years of the twentieth century.

2 Watercolor and inking brushes come in a variety of lengths and widths, and a numbering system was developed to order their sizes. The numbers range from 30/0 for the smallest brush to 30 for the largest. The numbers are relative since the sizes are not standard among all manufacturers.

3 Carbon paper is coated on one side with dry ink. When placed between two clean sheets of paper and pressure is applied to the top, a duplicate is created on the bottom sheet; show card colors are opaque watercolors that come in strong, matte colors, ideal for window bills and other forms of advertising. They are popularly called poster paints.

4 There is a distinction between a letterpress and letterpress printing. The former is a small tabletop screw press (often called a copying press) used from about 1780 to copy letters onto sheets of thin, damp paper by applying pressure to a freshly inked missive. It could also be used for block printing as Rice notes (p. 25). Letterpress printing is the name given to the printing process that utilizes inked relief images (originally woodcuts) and raised type to imprint words and designs on paper. It was introduced into Europe by Johannes Gutenberg around 1450 using the first screw printing press adapted from agricultural presses.

5 Hosho, made from the kozo plant, is a type of handmade paper from Japan, first manufactured in the sixteenth century as a luxury item reserved for important documents. Its high quality, strength, and absorbency have long been admired by block printmakers.

6 Battleship linoleum is a special heavy-gauge linoleum originally commissioned by the US Navy and used on warships until World War II. Its thickness, pliability, and gray color were well suited for linocutting.

7 Flattine derived its name from the product's use as a "flattening" or "matting" agent to reduce the reflectivity of inks. While Flattine is no longer manufactured, other matting agents are commercially available.

8 A clothes wringer was a ubiquitous washtub adjunct through the 1950s, when it was made increasingly obsolete by electric and gas dryers. Composed of two superimposed wooden rollers activated by a hand crank, the wringer removed excess moisture from wet clothes when pressed between the rollers. The clothes were then hung out to dry. It made a handy and serviceable press for thin, unmounted linoleum blocks.

CHAPTER III
SELECTING THE BLOCK

At the present time many different materials are used in place of wood for block-printing purposes. Wood was, of course, the material used by the originators of this art; and there are still some who contend that only wood is legitimate. The old-timers used cherry, boxwood, pear, and other smooth-grained woods that the modern craftsman finds it difficult to obtain. The author has found that three-ply red gumwood gives good results. It has a very fine grain and cuts crisply.

Linoleum is a good substitute for wood, especially for the beginner. It has no grain, therefore, it may be cut readily in any direction. It does not splinter and it prints a smooth, even tone.

Linoleum may be used either mounted or unmounted. It depends entirely on how the printing is to be done. When the blocks are to be printed by means of a clothes wringer or on an etching press, they must be unmounted because the space between the rollers is not sufficient to admit mounted blocks. However, for hand rubbing as the Japanese do with a burnisher, called a baren, or for printing in a common letterpress or a commercial printing press, it is quite necessary, in order to get the best results, that the blocks be mounted type-high (.9186 inch). Mounted linoleum blocks, type-high, with whitened surfaces may now be purchased in various sizes. If you mount your own blocks, use strong glue to stick the linoleum to the wood; then place the blocks in a letterpress to dry. Medium-thick linoleum, unpatterned, is most suitable for mounting purposes. If the linoleum is to be used unmounted, it should be ¼ inch thick. For this purpose "battleship" linoleum is best.

It is important that all blocks of a series, where color is to be used, be cut exactly the same size so that they will register properly in the printing.

Rubber mounted on wood blocks presents a delightful surface for cutting or engraving. The tools, of course, in this case must be kept very sharp at all times, if good clean-cut lines are to be obtained.

Commercial printing establishments have brought to the author's notice, at various times, new composition blocks with delightfully smooth surfaces. These print very smoothly, but they have the disadvantage of hard surfaces to cut and are usually so high priced that they are beyond the reach of the average student.

Bird Design—Student

CHAPTER IV

CUTTING THE BLOCK

After oiling with olive oil, Vaseline, or linseed oil, the back of the design glued on the block, wipe the surface with a soft rag to remove any superfluous oil.

A solid, flat table or a drawing board resting on a table makes a substantial surface on which to rest the block while carving it. Two strips of wood, like an L, nailed on the board hold the linoleum block in place while carving, and prevent its slipping. This allows both hands to be free while carving. Some craftsmen prefer a wooden device known as a bench hook.[1]

Tools must be kept sharp at all times. Dull tools merely chew the linoleum. A set of small slipstones and some 3-in-One oil should be kept on hand for frequent use.[2] If blocks are cut in cold weather, warm them over a gas or oil stove. The linoleum becomes less brittle and cuts more readily.

The cutting tool is held in the right hand with the ball of the handle in the palm, and the right side of the handle gripped firmly, but not too tightly with the third, fourth, and fifth fingers. For further control, place the forefinger along the top of the cutting shaft and the thumb at the left of the shaft. Or one can hold the head of the handle against the inside of the little finger and the cutting shaft between the thumb and other fingers. In cutting always push the tool away from you.

Cutting the block is not determined by rules but by individual ingenuity and experience. If you use the following suggestions as a general procedure, you can increase your skill by practice and experiment. With a knife, cut around the white areas of the design at an oblique angle to the line. This gives greater strength to lines, not having much thickness to support themselves under heavy pressure. The surplus parts are next removed with a ¼-inch gouge or a No. 8 carving tool.[3] All material between lines should be scooped out clean, so that the paper will not touch bottom in the printing and pick up stray and objectionable spots of ink. Fine lines within the design are cut out with the veining tool. Apply sufficient weight to the tools to make the cuts penetrate through the filling to the burlap. If the cutting is carefully done, the large masses may be removed from the burlap with little difficulty.

The tools may be described as U-shaped veiners, V-shaped veiners, gouges, and chisels.[4] Take a piece of scrap linoleum and experiment freely with all these tools and thereby discover your own preferences. Veining tools are used for cutting close to the lines or masses of the design and may thus be considered outlining tools, while gouges and chisels are better suited for quickly removing large masses of the background.

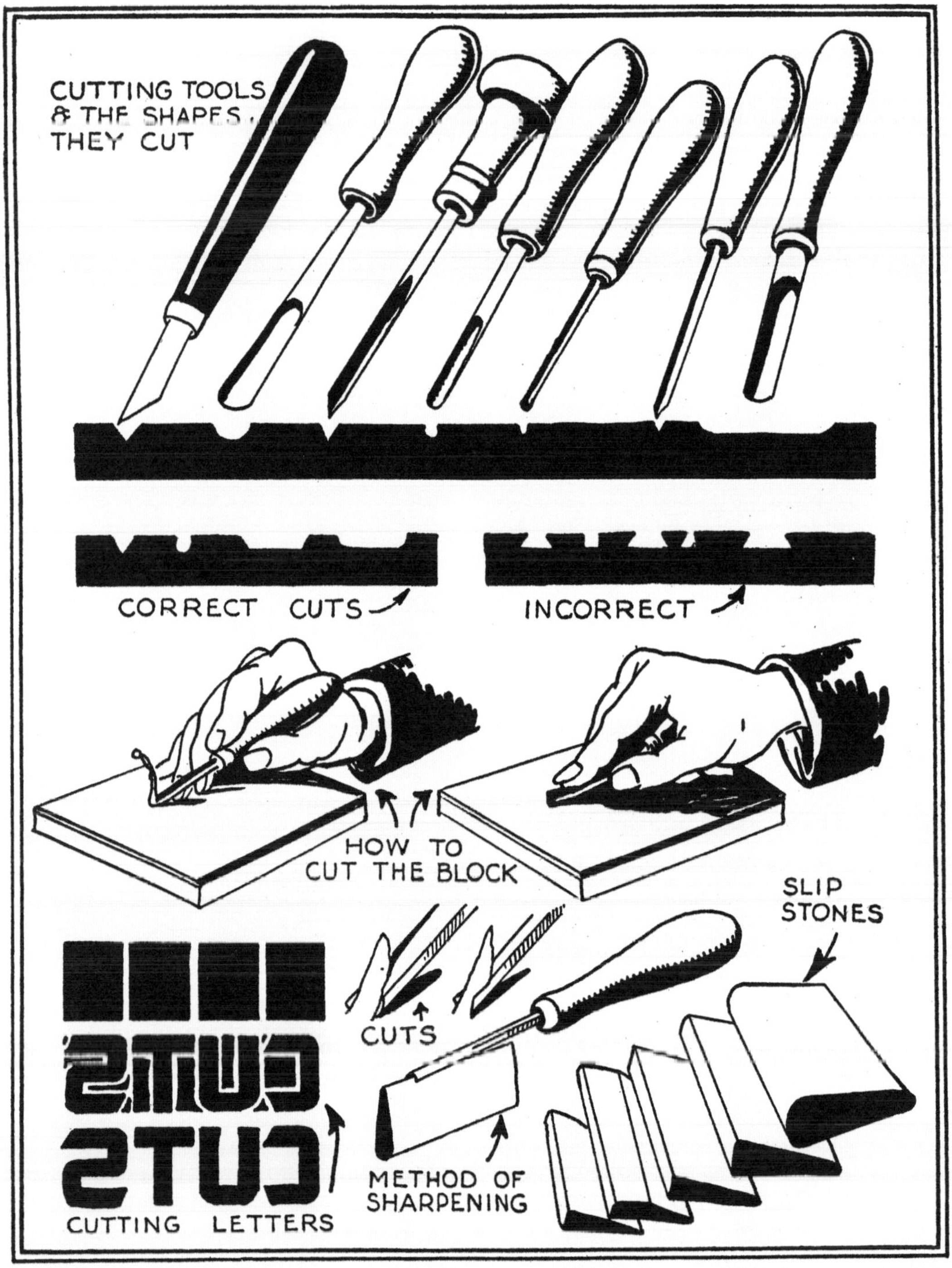

Tools and Method of Carving

Cutting the block with a knife gives a certain severity to the work. The veining tool, on the other hand, produces more freedom because of its shape. This is very desirable and artistic for certain subjects. Many craftsmen prefer the gouge cut to the knife cut, but all tools have their followers. In fact, all types may be used on the same block without destroying the character of the technique.

There is no special part of any line on which one should commence cutting (or engraving). The craftsman feels for himself where he may best begin. The tool is propelled along the guide lines of the design, away from the operator. The angle of the tool and the block is best determined by the lines to be cut and their direction. The depth to which the tool cuts into the surface of the linoleum will decide the width of the engraved channel, which eventually appears as white in the print. If one strains the tool to its utmost depth, the top of the sides of the V-shaped gouge is apt to jar and bruise the edges of the line cut and cause ragged edges.

With the gouge tools, a trench may be cut with one single action of the tool. This is an advantage over knife cutting which demands two actions to make one trench. Gouge work is therefore more speedy than knife work in its results at all times. On the other hand, gouge work, in the hands of an unskilled workman, loses much of its character. Curves and angles require the utmost care in cutting. Pivoting the block works better than turning the tool in cutting curves or angles.

NOTES

1 A bench hook is a simple worktable device. It is constructed of a short board to which two transverse pieces are affixed: one on the top end (the "stop") and the other on the underside of the opposite end (the "hook"). The hook is placed against the edge of the worktable while the object to be worked is held firmly in place against the stop.

2 3-in-One is a multipurpose oil first formulated in 1894 as a lubricant for bicycle chains and is still in production. The "3" in its name reflects its combined ability to prevent rust, lubricate, and clean.

3 Woodcarving tools are traditionally numbered from 1 to 11 to indicate the "sweep" (curvature) of their blades. Number 1 is flat, number 2 is slightly curved, and so on up to number 11, which is a U shape.

4 A veiner is a small tool that carves fine V-shaped or U-shaped grooves in wood or linoleum. Its name comes from its historical use for engraving the delicate veins of foliage.

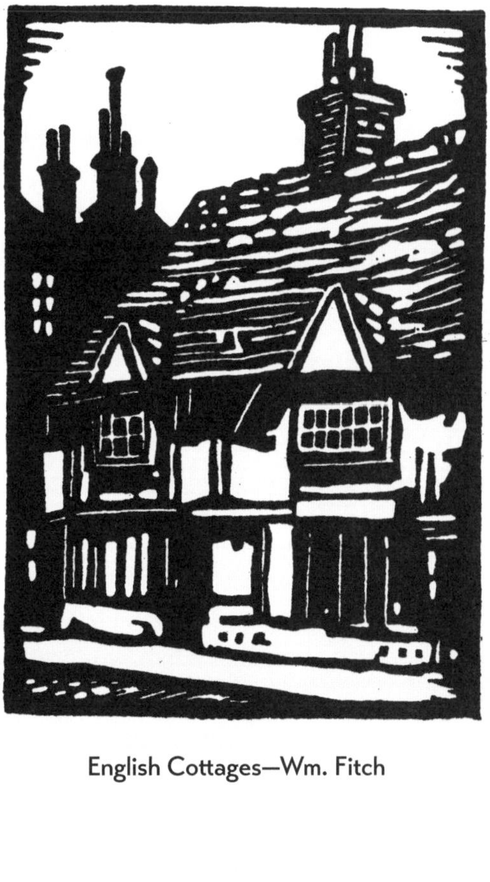

English Cottages—Wm. Fitch

CHAPTER V
METHODS OF PRINTING FROM BLOCKS

When the paper design is removed and the cut block dried with a soft cloth, it is ready for inking to make the first proof. To do this, take a palette knife and spread a small quantity of printers' ink (which comes in tubes like oil paint) on a pane of glass which has a sheet of white paper pasted on the underside. With the printers' roller or brayer, distribute the ink on the glass by rolling the brayer back and forth until the ink becomes a thin film. Then roll the inked brayer over the engraved surface of the block (which may be wood or linoleum – the method is the same) first back and forth, then crosswise.

The proofing may be done by laying the paper on the inked block and rubbing on the back of it with a burnisher, or baren, as the Japanese call it. A baren is a disk of pasteboard in which is coiled a braided mat, over which is stretched bamboo leaves with their ends neatly twisted and tied together over the top. Barens cannot be purchased in this country, so consequently one will have to be on the lookout for a substitute.[1] Cornhusks may take the place of the bamboo leaf; the texture of both is somewhat similar. Other substitutes successfully used are wooden, glass, or metal caster cups, or a hardwood roller such as wallpaper hangers use.

Proofs may be pulled on ordinary white tissue paper. Then use these proofs to make any needed corrections on the block – such corrections include ragged edges, thick lines, and high points in the nonprinting areas – before starting to make the final prints on Japanese paper. Serious mistakes will necessitate a new block. If a minor error has been made in a wood block, cut away the spot and insert a wooden plug or fill in the miscuts with wood filler and smooth with fine sandpaper. In the case of linoleum, a new piece can be glued into place. The corrected block is termed the "key block." The next step is printing.

Various methods of printing from blocks are used. The simplest methods – by hand or foot pressure – will be described first. Hand printing is like taking proofs. A sheet of Hosho paper is placed in position against the guides or stops which have been provided on the inked block. The sheet is then covered with thin paper and gently rubbed with a baren or some other burnisher. In printing on textiles the solid blow of a hammer is used instead of a burnisher. Foot pressure is practical for large blocks. A pile of blankets is laid on the floor, the textile next, and the inked block (facedown) on top of this. The feet are then used to give the necessary pressure. Printing with presses requires more equipment but less skill and care.

The clothes wringer makes a serviceable printing press when small, unmounted

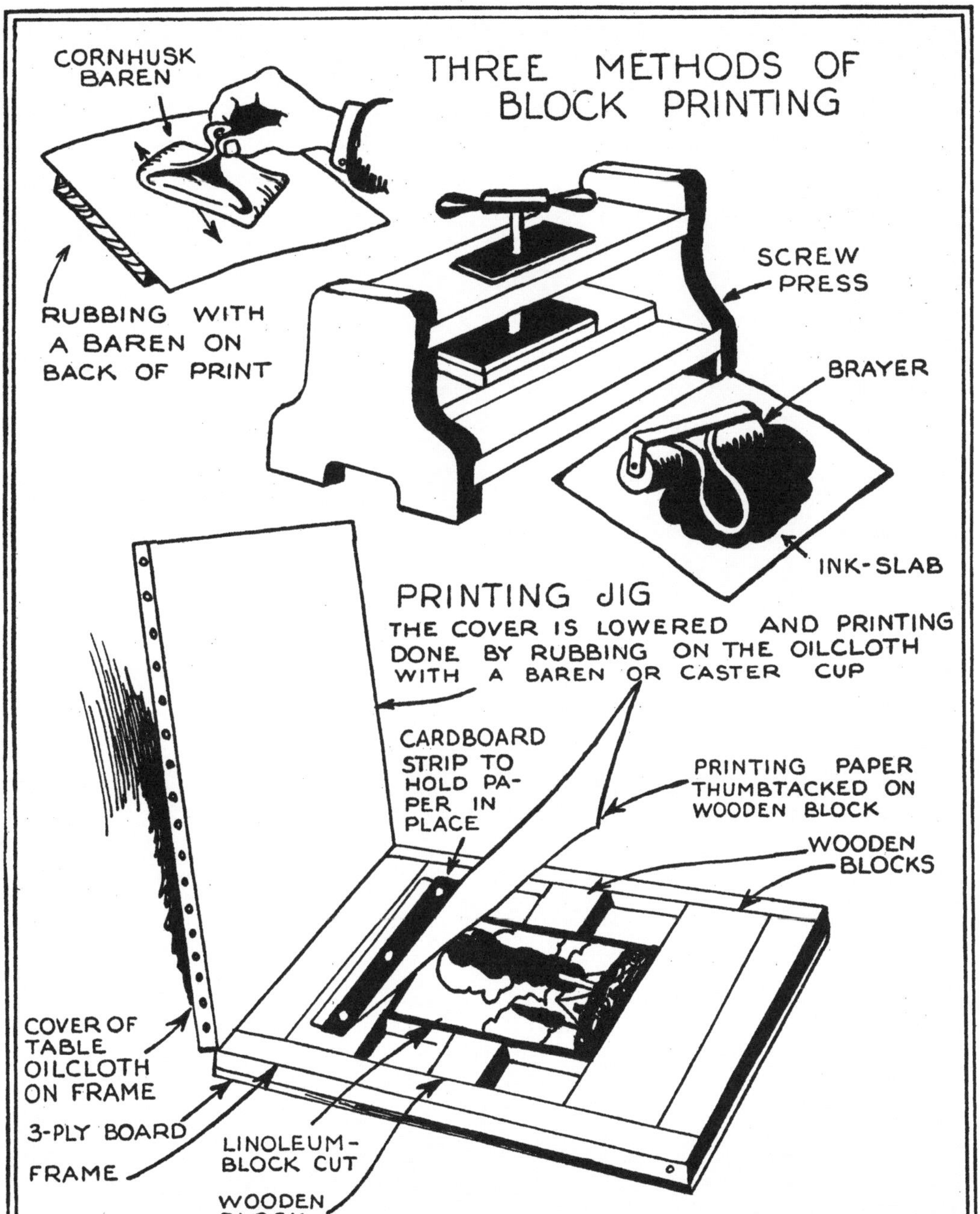

Printing Equipment

blocks are used. If you own an etching press, you will find it ideal for block printing. An old-fashioned letterpress, if you are fortunate enough to find one, is admirable for making block prints. Here again one is limited in the size of one's prints to the size of the bed and plate, or of the letterpress.

For prints, a printing frame is practical and is easy to construct. It consists of two wooden frames hinged together. The upper one has a piece of table oilcloth or artists' canvas stretched on it and the lower frame is nailed onto a drawing board. The lower frame serves as a device to lock the block tightly in place by means of wooden wedges.

To print, the block is inked in the frame, a sheet of paper is laid on it, the canvas-covered frame (or lid) lowered, and the impression made by rubbing vigorously on the back of canvas with any one of the burnishers mentioned above. With the printing frame there is no danger of the paper skidding or tearing holes in it.

The beginner should be content with printing from the key blocks only. Color printing which requires several blocks is better suited to students who have had considerable practice, since a knowledge of color harmony and registration of the multiple blocks requires a very steady hand and considerable experience.

Of the various papers used in printing, nothing works quite so satisfactorily as Hosho, a Japanese paper which may be obtained of Japanese dealers in the larger cities.[2] The absorbent quality of Japanese papers enables them to pick up all the ink in the printing. Paper may be used dry or dampened – a matter of individual preference. Absorbent papers always work best; therefore, avoid either very rough or glazed surfaced papers.

For school printing and gift cards, the tinted construction papers which come in a great variety of colors print very well (when dampened by sponging and kept between wet blotters) and are quite inexpensive. They may be purchased at the five-and-ten-cent stores or at firms manufacturing art supplies for schools.

NOTES

1 Japanese-made barens were probably unavailable in the United States after July 1941 (the year Rice's book was published), when virtually all commercial traffic between the two countries ceased in a prelude to the United States entering World War II.

2 Rice obtained his Japanese papers from small shops in San Francisco's Chinatown.

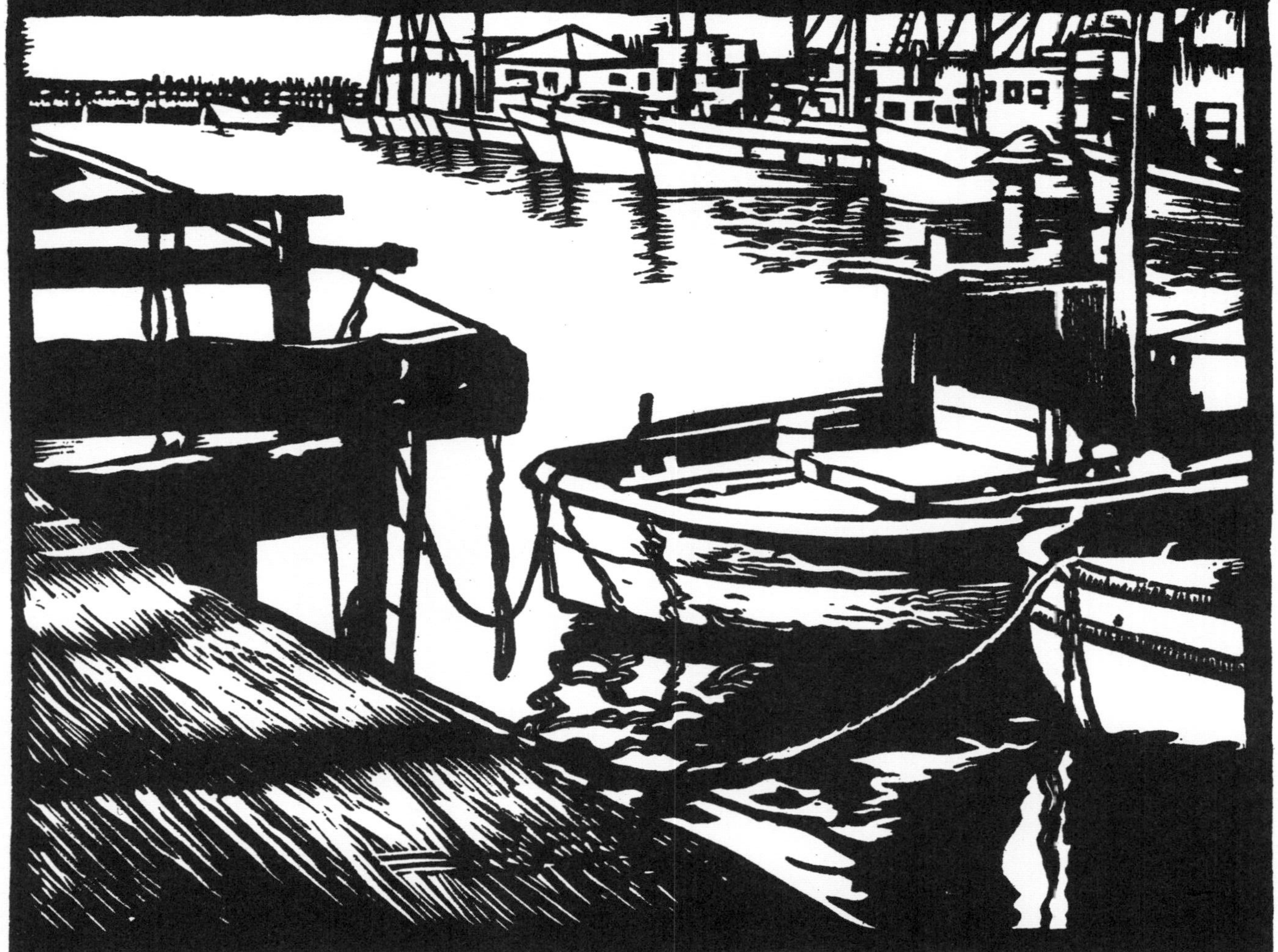

Fisherman's Wharf—San Francisco

CHAPTER VI

COLOR PRINTING

The One-Block Method

The earliest method of coloring block prints was to make proofs of the dark outlines and to fill in the white spaces by hand with watercolors. But today all methods of color printing require that the colors be painted on the print not by hand, but by making one impression upon another until the picture is complete. Of various methods the one-block – wood or linoleum – method is an interesting way to make block prints.[1] For wood blocks either watercolors or inks with an oil base may be used, but for linoleum, only inks with an oil base are suitable. Prints made by this method have a white outline around each color, giving them a "postery" or decorative effect.

With a suitable subject having been chosen – landscape, bird, fruit, flowers, or figures – the subject is penciled to the desired size on manila paper. The design is made so that the various portions are separated by a white line. The study should be treated strictly as a design, and the background spaces kept in pleasing relation to the objects in the composition.

Next lay a sheet of tracing paper on the design and ink the outlines with a Speedball pen (a soft lead pencil or crayon may serve as a substitute).[2] Rule a ¼-inch borderline around the edge of the wood block, which may be white pine, sugar pine, or three-ply wood, and then trace the design.

After the design is traced by rubbing on the reverse side with a soft pencil, the cutting begins. To cut a wood block, a single-edged razor blade is very good. If battleship linoleum is used, a veiner will work very effectively. A V-shaped trough or canal is cut along the outline and the material carefully removed from the groove. This groove may be about 1⁄16 inch in width, but it may vary in places where accents are needed.

After dampening the block with a wet sponge, it is ready to use. Fasten the block securely to a drawing board with strips of gummed paper tape held down with thumbtacks. The "printing frame" is also suited for making prints by the one-block method.

Now lay the paper – Japanese Hosho paper works best and has a certain artistic quality not found in the cheaper papers – down smoothly on the block and run the hand all around it, forming a crease that will register accurately each time the paper is lifted and put back in place. This forms a perfect keying and allows a critical study to be made of the print while it progresses.

Watercolors are next painted on a small area of the block and the paper is brought down over the block and rubbed on the back with a burnisher or baren. The paper is then lifted and another spot painted, and so on until the print is complete. To strengthen a color one should wait until the first printing is dry, otherwise the printing paper becomes too wet and sometimes tears. Moreover, the result will lack that particular vibration quality which is the charm of this type of printing.

If printing inks with an oil base are used instead of watercolors, the inks may be diluted with a few drops of turpentine or kerosene so that they may be applied to the block with brushes. Rollers cannot be used for applying the inks in the one-block method. Sable brushes both flat and round are quite suitable.

NOTES

1 The single-block color woodblock print, sometimes called a white-line woodcut or Provincetown print, was popularized in the United States by a group of painter-printmakers who began working in this shortcut to color block printing in Provincetown, Massachusetts, in 1915. However, Rice was introduced to this method through the work of early Japanese printmakers that he saw at the Panama-Pacific International Exposition that same year.

2 The Speedball pen was introduced by the C. Howard Hunt Pen Company in 1915. The pen came with a variety of removable nibs that were suited to various types of lettering.

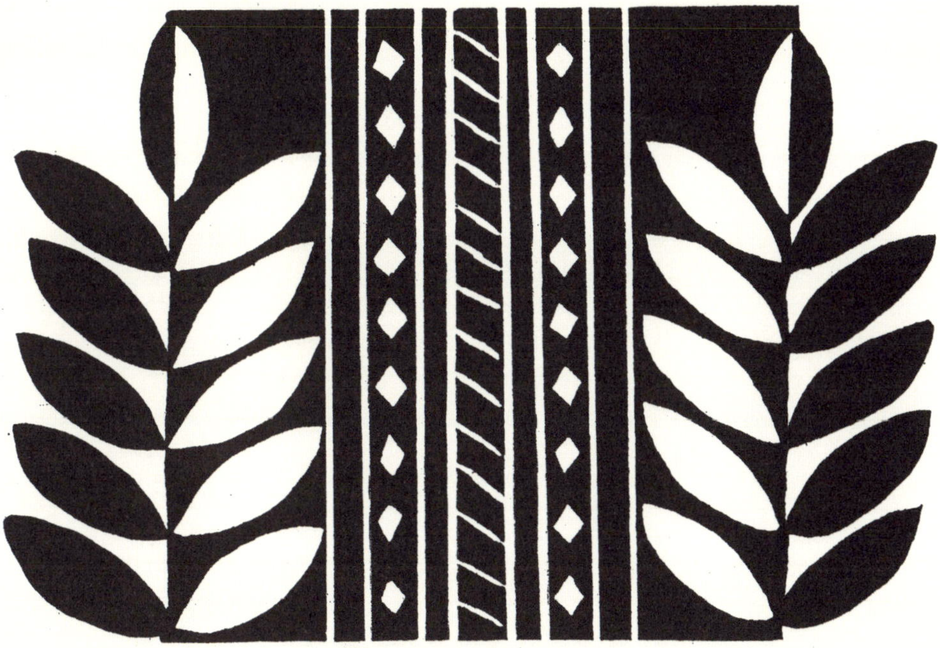

Allover Design—Student

CHAPTER VII

COLOR PRINTING

The Two-Block Method or Tint-Block Method

The two-block method comprises a key block in dark outlines and masses and a tint block to print the color. The key block which contains the outlines of the drawing is cut as previously described, and a proof of it is struck off on tracing paper. This wet proof is laid facedown on a clean block of the same size as the key block. Rub the back of the proof vigorously with a spoon or burnisher and remove. The result of that offset on this second block will be a reversed impression of the original design. When this is thoroughly dry, remove with a knife and a veining tool or V-shaped gouge the areas intended to print as white spaces.

After the tint block is cleaned with a rag and kerosene, it is ready for the color. Flat and round sables of various sizes may be used to apply the colors which may be thinned out a trifle with linseed oil or kerosene. The roller may be used when only one or a graded tint is desired. Very pleasing results may thus be obtained with simplified color.

To print more than one color, it is necessary to make several proofs from the key block and either "offset" them or glue them facedown on clean blocks alike in size for as many colors as are needed. However, if the color areas are widely separated and the inks are applied with brushes instead of a roller, one block may serve to print several colors.

Now mark the areas which are to print the color. Then cut away the rest of the block, but not the corners because they are necessary to register the block on all other impressions.

Additional information concerning the inking or coloring of tint blocks may be found useful. The inking may be accomplished by means of a brayer, or by means of a flat, 3-inch sable brush. Suppose one wishes to use a graduated tint ranging from ivory to deep blue. First, mix separately the ivory and the deep blue with the palette knife. Then with a horizontal movement roll the ivory color about halfway down the block, clean the brayer, and, beginning at the bottom of the block, roll on the blue. Roll the blue upward until it meets and blends with the ivory without showing an abrupt line. For this type of blending the consistency of the inks should be rather heavy and sticky, just as they come from the tube. If one color is heavier or thicker than the other, they will not blend satisfactorily. Experiments alone can determine the proper adjustment.

The brush method differs in that one is obliged to mix a bit of turpentine with the inks in order to brush them on the block and blend them properly. In this case the brush must be used with a horizontal stroke to obtain the desired effect.

For color printing, oil paints are never as satisfactory as the regular printing inks.

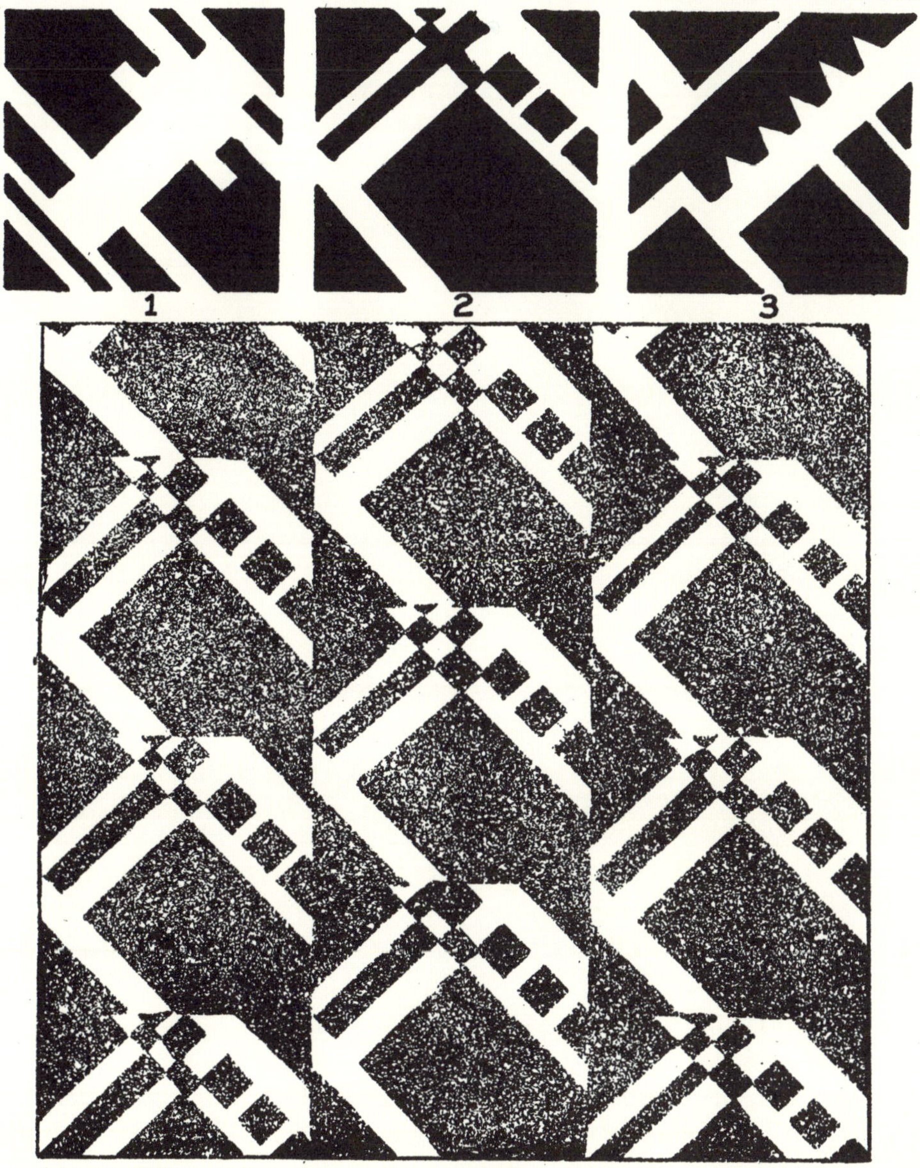

ALLOVER DESIGN PRINTED FROM LINOLEUM BLOCK NO. 2

The following colors are recommended for the beginner. Others may be added from time to time if desired.

1. White	5. Blue
2. Black	6. Green
3. Red	7. Violet (apt to be fugitive)
4. Yellow	

Orange is a useful color and can be easily made by mixing yellow and red together. A green can be made by mixing blue and yellow, but it is not so intense as a ready-made green. This is likewise true of violet, but one should beware of this latter color since it is not permanent. Black and red with a bit of yellow make several shades of brown. Magenta is a good color and, though lacking permanence, is sometimes useful in flower prints. Yellow ocher will be found useful for various color combinations. In making tints, one should begin with white and gradually add the dark color, mixing them with a palette knife until the desired tone is reached.

When the colors have been applied to the various blocks, the printing begins. The blocks are printed one at a time until lastly the key block (the dark-outline block) is printed over the other impressions and the print is completed.

Registering the blocks on the various imprints is not easy and different printers have their own way of accomplishing this operation. The Japanese printmakers have a very practical and simple way of registering their blocks. Considerable space is left on the top of the block for two register grooves or depressions cut like Ls. These must be uniformly cut and spaced on each color block, so that the paper will accurately hit the same and correct spot each time a new impression is made.

A simplification of the Japanese method may be made by following these directions. Three strips of wood are nailed on a drawing board so as to form three sides of a hollow square or rectangle which will exactly fit the block. These strips should be slightly lower than the thickness of the linoleum block, whether it be mounted type-high or unmounted. Another strip of wood the same height and slightly shorter than the width of the drawing board may be nailed in place some distance away from the other strips. This is to hold the printing paper, which is thumbtacked securely to it to prevent sliding. A strip of heavy cardboard under the thumbtacks prevents tearing the paper and holds the paper more firmly. The printing in this case is done with the baren. A sheet of tracing paper laid on the back of the printing paper prevents the operator tearing holes in the print.

When a second or third block is to be used to print colors, it is inked with the brayer in the usual manner, the paper gently lifted back, and the respective blocks slipped in position. The printing is then continued until all the color impressions are made. This form of registry may be regarded as reliable and safe but only on condition that the entire set of blocks is absolutely alike in size. If they vary, registry will not result.

After the prints are completed, they should be hung up with thumbtacks or spread out on a table to dry. This usually requires about twenty-four hours, but some inks dry more rapidly than others.

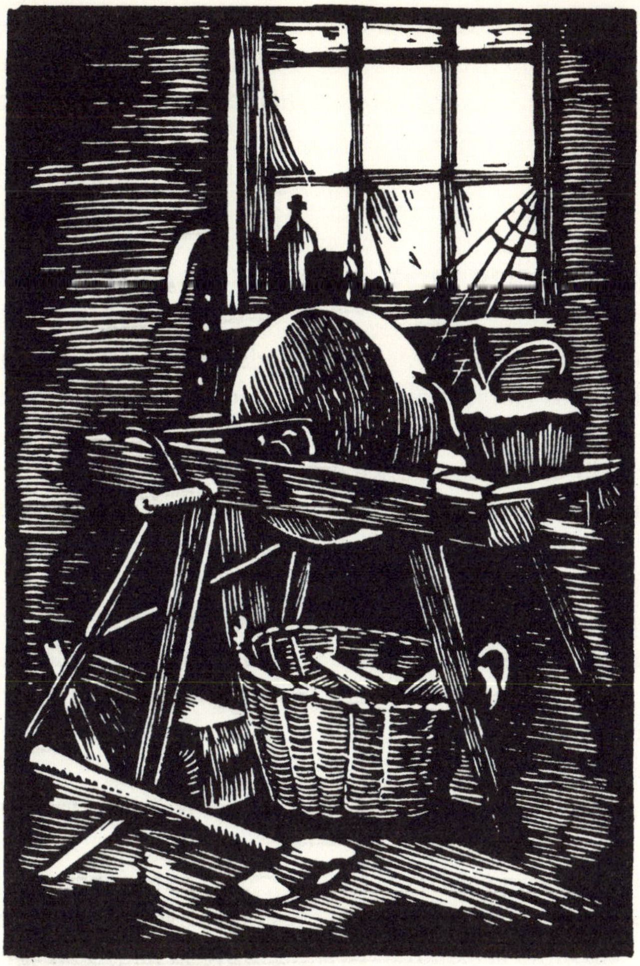

Grandpa's Grindstone

Wet prints should never be laid on top of each other, lest they offset and ruin the appearance of the work.

Prints made by either of the mentioned methods show more variety than those inked more mechanically with a roller and printed on a commercial press. However, these methods are more tedious and are better suited to the professional artist than to the amateur, or even to the commercial printer.

The viewpoint of the artist differs from that of the commercial printer. In hand printing, each print has a beauty and individuality of its own. The aim is not to produce editions in large quantities, all alike and uniform, but to obtain slight variations which give a personal character to each print.

Color block printing taken seriously is an artists' craft, like etching or lithography. To make a success of this craft one must have imagination, ideas, knowledge, and, above all, unlimited patience. The free inking of the blocks, the judgment of pressure in making the imprints no less than the creation of the design and color scheme, tend to demand the artists' utmost creative effort.

The making of color prints of this type is essentially a painter's performance. There is a great fascination about color experimentation. The real pleasure comes from seeing the same subject appear in different colors, the design gaining in interest with each new color scheme. Wonderful color effects may be obtained by continual experiments. It would almost seem, sometimes, that no block has ever spoken its last word when it comes to its final color scheme.

The owner of a block print possesses an original work of art direct from the hand of the artist. Every proof pulled from a set of hand-cut blocks for a given subject is an original thus differing from a facsimile reproduction of a picture. The latter is produced by photomechanical means. No matter how faithfully the original may thus be copied, the prints are mechanical reproductions nonetheless.

An edition of prints means the entire number of proofs the artist intends to pull from a block (or set of color blocks). Editions run from 25 to 100 or more, and each print is numbered in the order of its being printed. For example, say the edition is 100, the first print would be marked in pencil on the lower margin next to the title thus 1/100, the second print 2/100, and so on. The artist's signature is also written in pencil on the lower right-hand margin.

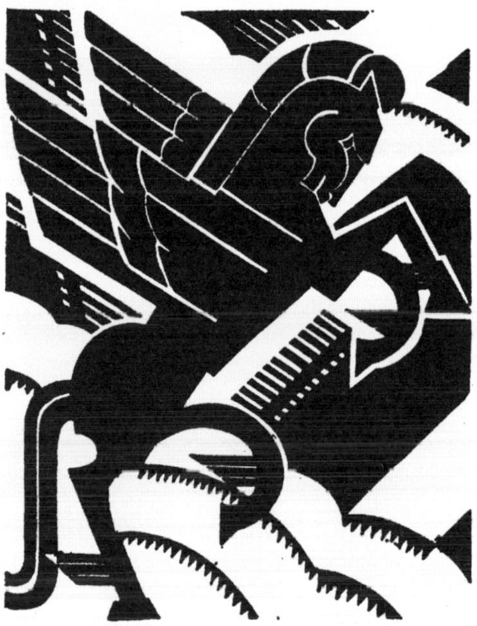

Allover Design—Student

CHAPTER VIII

WHITE SILHOUETTES OF NATURAL FORMS

A block of battleship linoleum is best for this problem. It may be whitened with a thin coating of poster paint to make the design stand out more clearly. The size may be whatever the student wishes.

Before beginning this problem, specimens of leaves, ferns, or sprays of vines and grasses should be gathered, laid between blotters or folded newspapers, and put under some weight or in a letterpress. When the sprays are dry, they may be shifted about the block until a pleasing space arrangement is obtained. Sometimes a little pruning of the spray will do wonders to the composition. When the composition seems to be entirely satisfactory, pin the leaves and stems securely to the surface of the block. The pins will do no harm, since they are pressed into the parts of the design that will be cut away.

Next dip a toothbrush in India ink or black poster paint and jerk it briskly over a knife blade, using a forward motion only. This is known commonly as spatterwork. The brush sends a fine spray over all the specimen and the background spaces of the block. After lifting the specimen from the block, there remains a white pattern on a dark background.

When the block is dry, cut away the light spaces (unspattered). The result, when the block is wiped and printed, will be a light silhouette on a dark background. The printing may be done on a letterpress, printing frame, or clothes wringer.

Very attractive prints may be made on toned paper, using green or violet inks. Matting the prints on a related or contrasting colored paper, allowing about ⅛ inch to show all around the print, will add considerably.

Prints of leaves, ferns, and grasses can be made real illustrative material in the botany classes by following the given instructions. At the same time, art principles should underlie the arrangement or composition of the specimens, the selection of the inks or papers for the color harmony of the printing, and lastly the mounting of the prints in an artistic "Nature Book" – a book that students may treasure for years to come.

Another type of printing from nature is to ink pressed natural specimens with a roller or brayer, using opposite or related colors for the color schemes, and to print directly from the natural sprays. After inking, arrange them artistically on the paper, face downward, cover with several blotters, and run them through the press – the etching press or clothes wringer is best for this type of printing.

Besides silhouette forms based on botanical specimens, the student will wish to try others, perhaps the human head and figure, animals, birds, and fishes. The method of procedure is simple. The

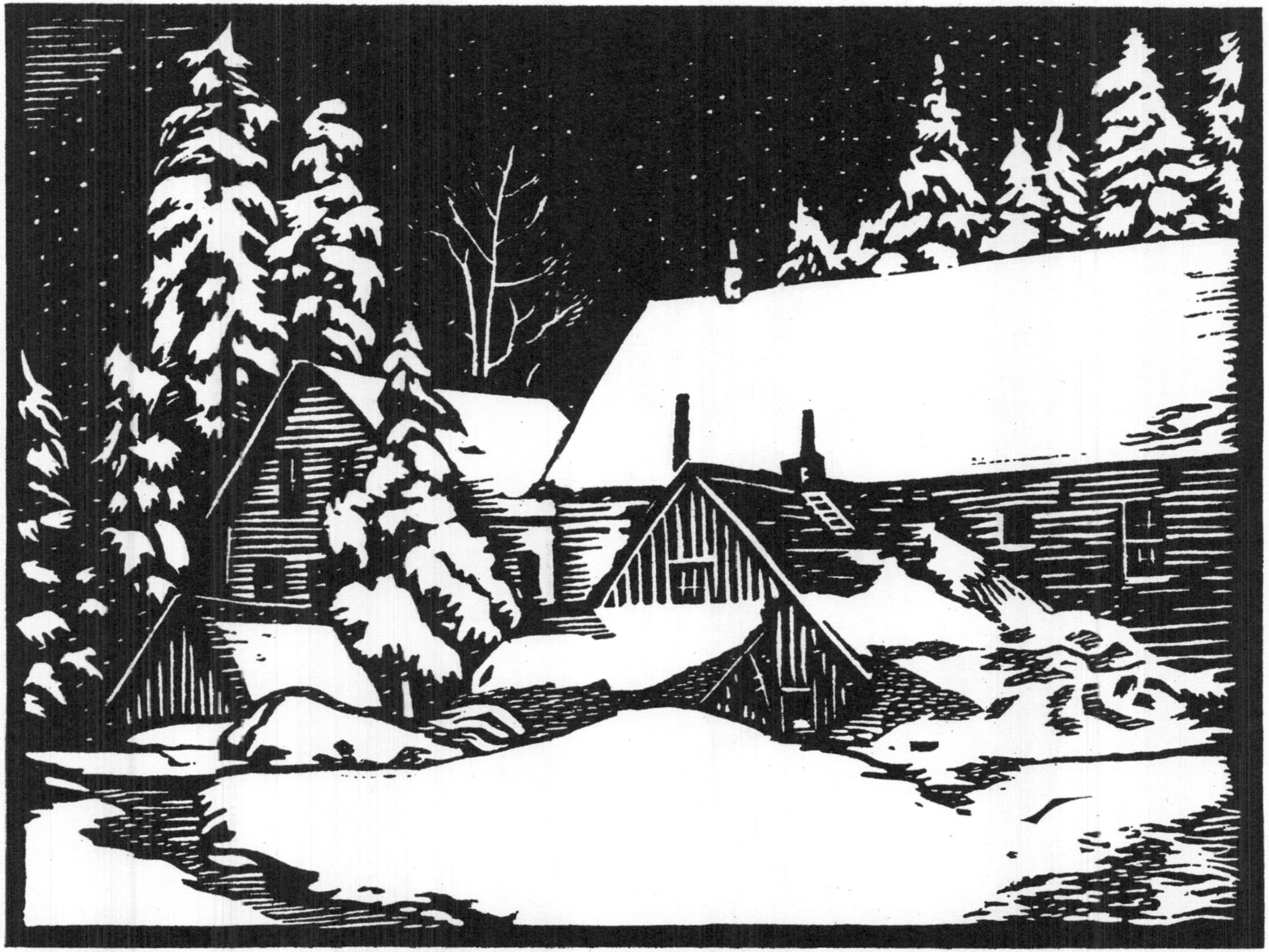

Snowstorm

first item to consider is the design, which may be sketched from living models or traced from photographs and transferred to the block in any of the ways previously described. If a dark silhouette against a white background is desired, one cuts away the background, leaving the drawing in relief. If a white silhouette is desired, one leaves the background in relief and gouges out the silhouette design, just as is done with the natural leaves and sprays described in the beginning of this chapter. Let it be stated again that the white silhouette is by far the easier of the two to cut, and, besides, the effect is more contrasting.

White silhouettes of fish against a dark background representing undersea effects are very forceful. For this you will have to refer to natural history plates in order to draw your fish correctly. Seaweeds, coral, or a few swirling lines across the design to suggest the motion of the water may be used to break up the background spaces. Designs of this type may be printed in deep blues, greens, or red-browns on cream-colored paper. No borderlines are necessary and the design runs to the very edge of the block.

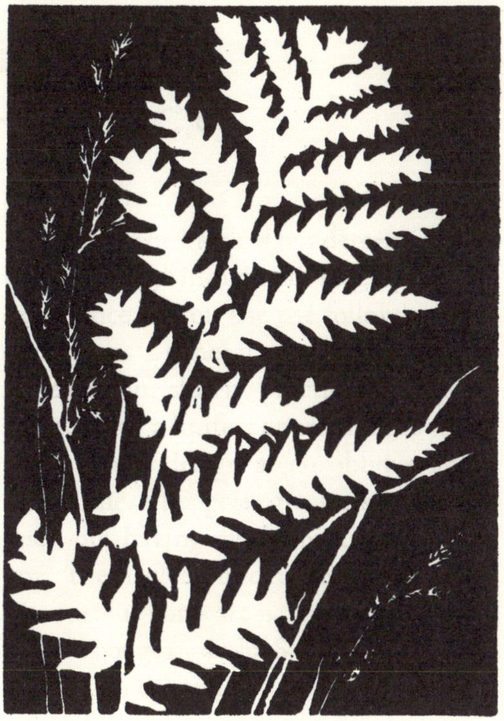

Plant Silhouette—Student

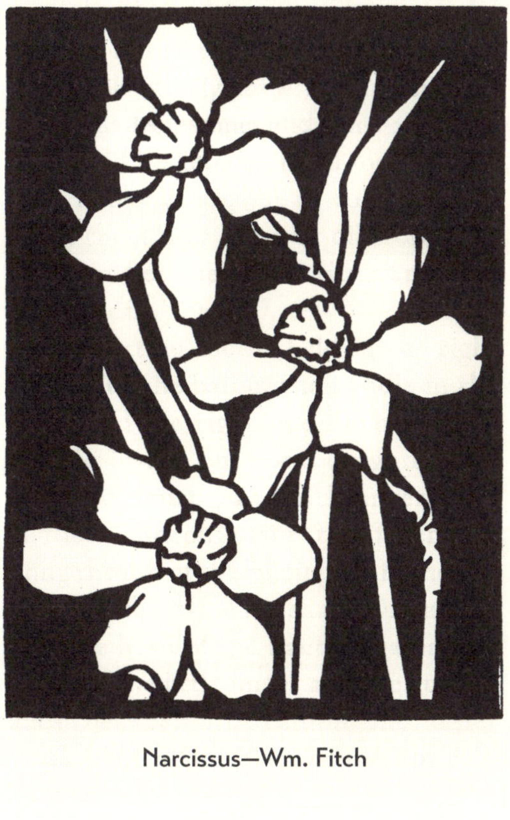

Narcissus—Wm. Fitch

A BLOCK LETTER EASY TO CUT

ABCDEFGHI
JKLMNOPQ
RSTUVW
XYZ
1234567890

Simple Letters

CHAPTER IX

LETTERING SUITABLE FOR BLOCK PRINTING

Although a knowledge of lettering is very essential to a block printer, the student need not be a specialist in this art. If one masters a few plain styles – for example, the single-stroke letter which is not difficult to cut with a veining tool, or a plain block letter commonly known as the Gothic letter – he will be amply equipped to letter gift cards, posters, etc. Script letters might also be included, but any kind of fancy letters, as Old English, for instance, should not be attempted by the novice.

A single-stroke letter, whether it be script or the plainest of unshaded letters, is the simplest to cut on linoleum. When one tries to cut shaded letters, he finds himself in deep water. A white letter on a dark background is by far the easiest to cut, since it may be done with one of the smaller U-shaped gouges.

In cutting block letters, cut around the entire letter with a small U-shaped gouge before routing out the surrounding background. If one does not care for the severe accuracy of a formal letter, some freedom in the cutting may be employed, but irregularity is likely to result. In order to obtain precision in relief or raised letters, one must be careful to cut exactly along the traced lines. Usually a solid piece is cut by using four strokes of the veining tool. This ensures perfect corners. Better results will follow when one cuts the interior shapes of the letters first, such as the enclosed areas in A, O, Q, B, R, and P. Afterward clear away the space around the letters.

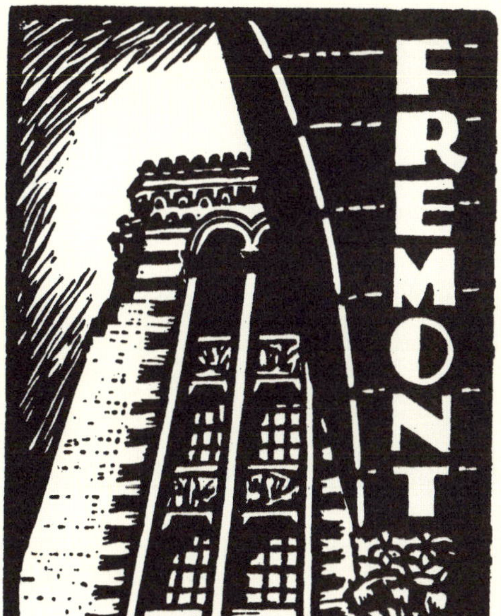

Maxwell Rice

LETTERS SUITABLE *for* LIGHT ON DARK

ABCDEFGHI
JKLMNOPQR
STUVWXYZ&
abcdefghijklm
nopqrstuvwxyz
1234567890

THICK AND THIN LETTERS EASY TO CUT IN LINOLEUM

ABCDEFGHIJ
KLMNOPQRS
TUVWXYZ&

Light on Dark Letters

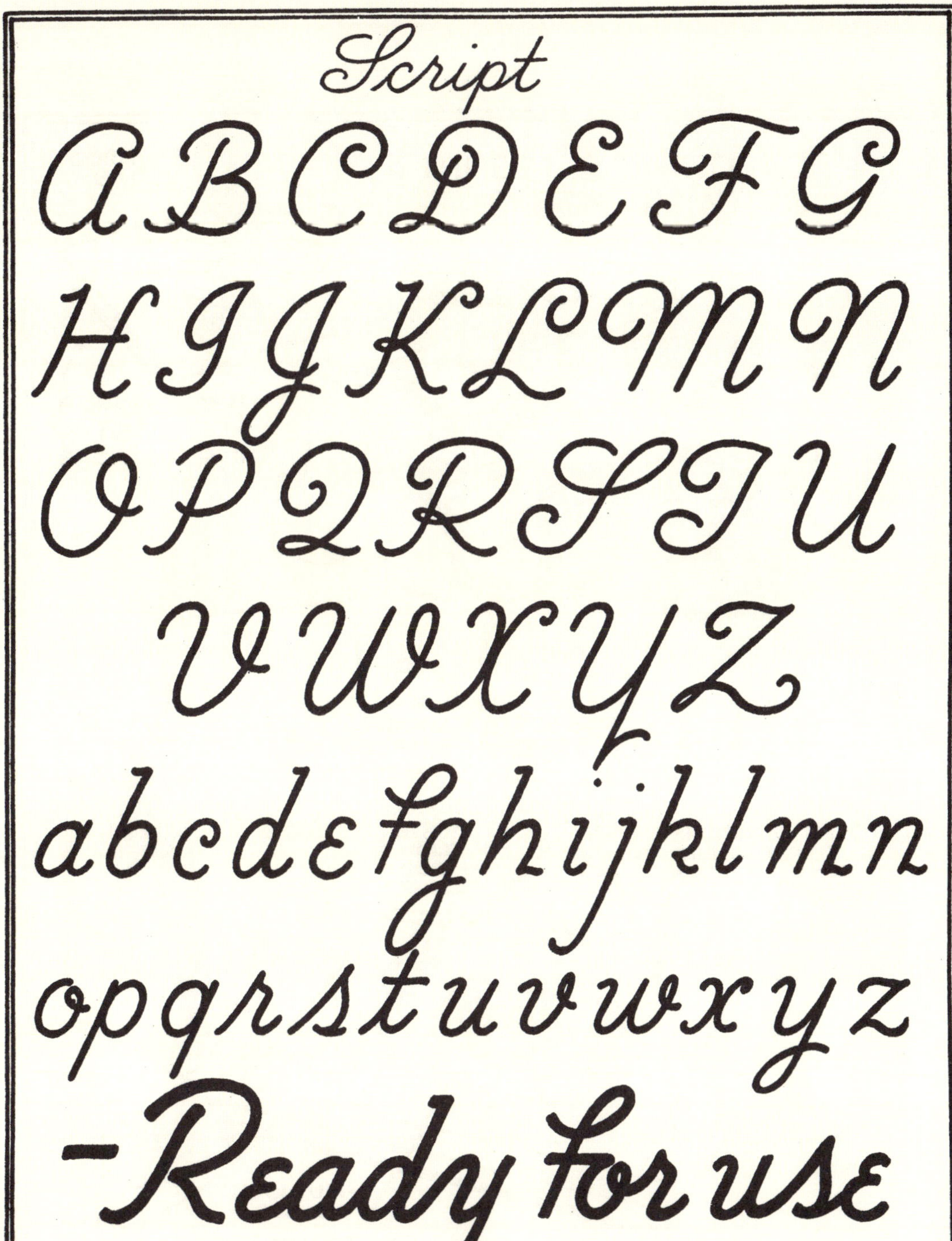

Script Lettering

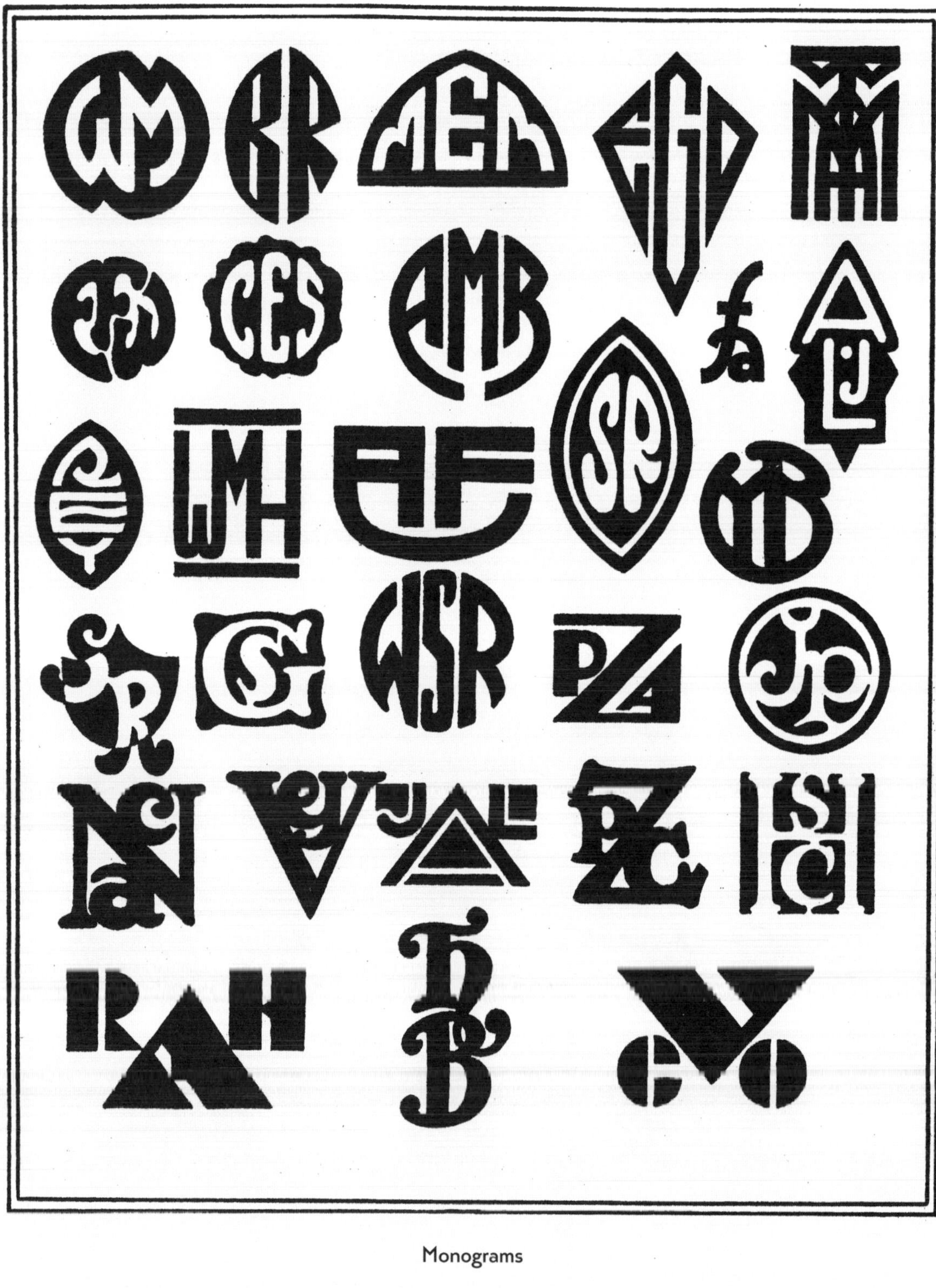

Monograms

CHAPTER X
MATTING AND FRAMING BLOCK PRINTS

Matting block prints requires considerable patience and a certain amount of mechanical dexterity. Sizes of mats in use are as follows: For exhibitions in print societies, 14¼ by 19¼-inch mats are the most popular, although occasionally 18 by 22-inch mats are allowed.[1] For home decoration, any appropriate size is permissible.

Material used for mats is cream-white bristol board (kid finish) but some prefer buckeye (ripple finish).[2] The backs of mats may be of a cheaper grade of material – Anchor Manila Tag, heavyweight, is most serviceable. Gummed paper or cloth tape serves as a hinge at the top and to "tip" the print to the back of the mat (inside, of course).[3]

Mats may be cut with a sharp knife or a razor blade. There should be about a ¼-inch space showing around the print on the top and sides, with a wider space at the bottom (about ½ inch to ⅜ inch). The opening cut into the mat should always be a trifle larger than the actual size of the print, so that a portion of the paper on which the print is made may be seen. Be sure to cut the opening in the mats so that the top and side margins are equal, and the bottom one somewhat wider. The reason for doing this is because the mechanical center of the mat is less pleasing to the eye than the optical center which is slightly above the actual center.

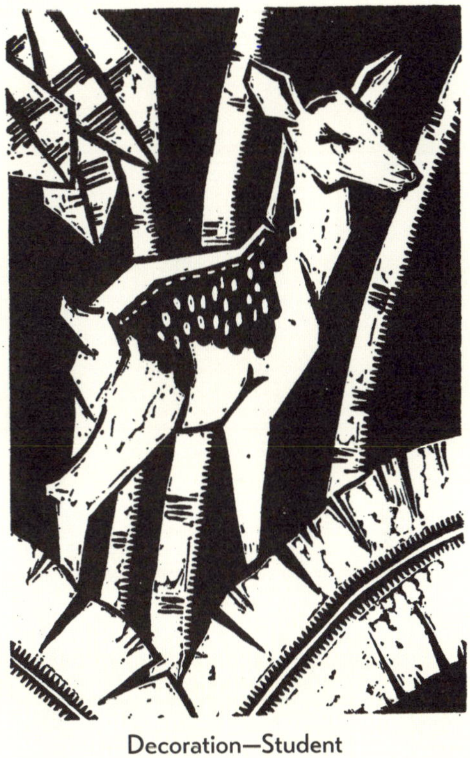

Decoration—Student

The title of the print and artist's signature are written in pencil just below the lower edge of the print itself.

Block prints are invariably framed with mats. There are exceptional cases, however, where mats are not used. Such instances are usually for prints of a purely decorative character, with strong colors and black backgrounds.

For such prints the most suitable frames are plain ones. A good, conservative molding is ¼ inch to ⅜ inch wide.

This is half round and may be in gray, brown, or black, or the natural wood color. A molding in black with a narrow edging of gold or silver is also in very good taste for framing block prints. The color scheme of the print should always decide which molding is the most harmonious.

NOTES

1 14¼ by 19¼ inches is still a standard mat measurement among American museums, though its origins are obscure.
2 Bristol board, reputedly named for its English city of origin, is a stiff, uncoated, machine-made pasteboard often preferred for illustration.
3 *Anchor, manila,* and *tag* are commercial or generic names for inexpensive, light cardboards often used for office files or posters. They also provided an adequate support for a print when hinged or taped to it. Today, neither they nor bristol board are recommended for matting fine prints due to the damaging acidity of the wood pulp used in their manufacture. Hinging with gummed or cloth tape, as Rice suggests, is also not recommended due to the difficulty of removal.

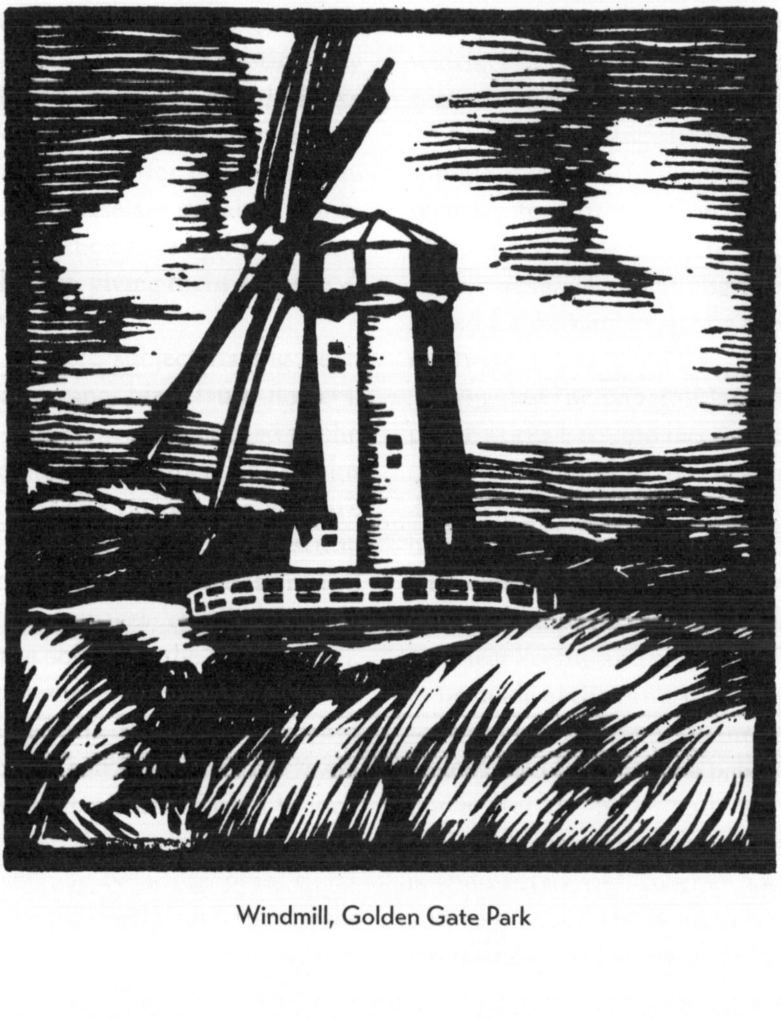

Windmill, Golden Gate Park

CHAPTER XI
CARE OF BLOCK-PRINTING EQUIPMENT

The care of tools and other block-printing equipment is of the greatest importance. Tools should be kept sharp at all times. Slipstones may be purchased to fit the curves and angles of the various carving tools. When Tif tools or Speedball cutters become dull, you will find it more economical to purchase a new set than to pay someone to sharpen them for you.[1]

The brayer or ink roller is an object requiring special care. It is composed of a gelatinous substance, therefore, the ink must never be allowed to dry on it. To clean it thoroughly, roll it briskly across newspapers until most of the ink is gone, then finish the job by wiping it with a rag saturated in kerosene. After cleaning, hang the roller on a nail on the wall so that the roller itself does not touch the wall surface. If it should touch, there is a tendency for it to flatten at the point of contact. In hot weather, rollers should be kept in a cool place when not in use. Never wash a gelatinous roller with water. Blocks should be wiped carefully with a kerosene rag as soon as the printing job is over.

Linoleum blocks that have become brittle may be cut with greater ease when the material is warm. In cold weather they should be warmed near a stove or radiator. It is surprising what a difference will be noticed in the cutting when this is done.

The ink slab should be cleaned with a rag and kerosene after the day's work is over. If you wish to save ink for later use, scrape it up with a palette knife, put it in a saucer, and fill the saucer with water. Inks thus treated may be kept fresh for several days.

Brushes, too, should be cleaned with kerosene immediately after using.[2] Oily rags should not be left lying carelessly around, since they might cause spontaneous combustion.

The care of prints is an important item to consider. The surface of the print should never be touched; neither should a print be picked up by one corner, especially the lower one, for this will cause a crease in the paper difficult to remove. It is well to mat prints as soon as they are dry and before showing them to anyone. Exhibitors should never punch holes in the mats to display them on a wall. Instead, paper fasteners should be glued to the backs of the mats. Unframed prints should not hang on walls or remain indefinitely without a glass protection. Neither should they be displayed in direct sunlight. There are no colors made that will stand up for any length of time, given that kind of treatment.

NOTES

1 Tif tools and Speedball cutters are linocutting tools consisting of a handle and a variety of removable blades. Tif (German abbreviation for *tiefenmesser*, or "deep knife") tools were manufactured by Heintze & Blanckertz of Berlin, Germany's first producer of dip pens. They progressively switched to linocutting tools beginning in the 1920s as ball pens supplanted nibs. Speedball cutters, like Speedball pens, were products of the C. Howard Hunt Pen Company, which became in 1936 the first large manufacturer of linoleum-block printing supplies. Speedball Art Products carries on the tradition.

2 Turpentine and mineral spirits are the most common ink and paint thinners today.

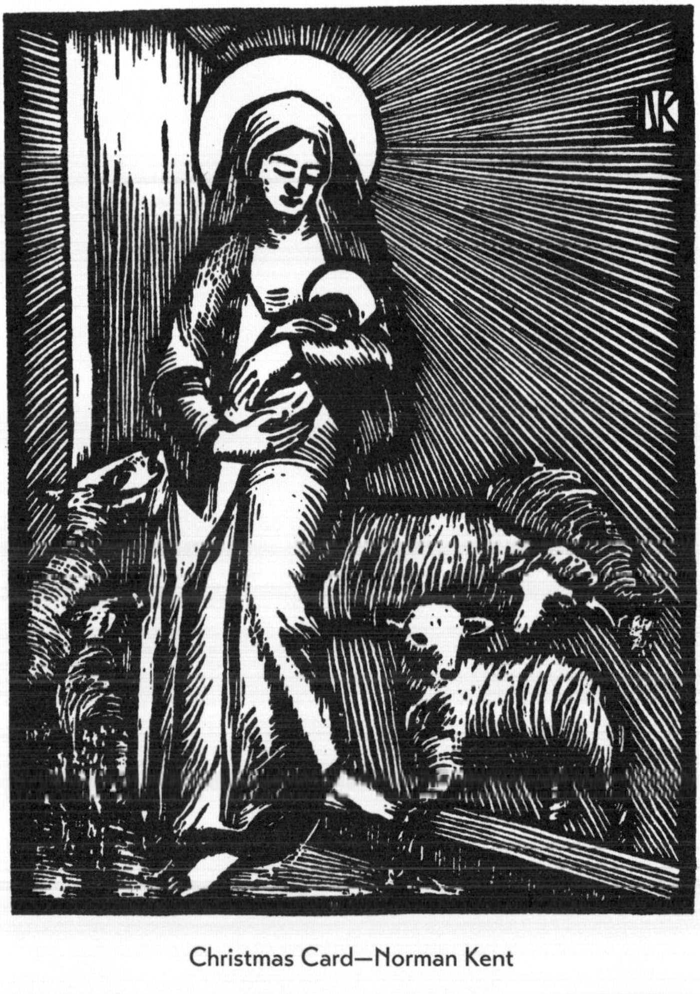

Christmas Card—Norman Kent

CHAPTER XII

GREETING CARDS — BOOKPLATES — LABELS — ETC.

Greeting cards which bear the touch of your personal craftsmanship are always more welcome to your friends than the "store" kind. The instructions given here can also be used for making personal bookplates with which to mark one's books.

The first thing necessary is to make a thoroughly good pencil sketch of whatever idea you have in mind. The illustrations which accompany this book are, of course, only suggestions. You will undoubtedly want to create your own greeting card, something individual and a little different. You might even be able to make a tracing from your favorite snapshot. Having made your sketch, lay a piece of tissue paper over it and trace it with brush and India ink. If you are not skillful at lettering, you had better leave a rectangular space open in your design, in which you can write your name or greeting. The average sizes of gift cards run from 3½ by 6½ inch to 4½ by 5½ inch.

When your design is complete, glue it facedown on a piece of battleship linoleum cut to the exact size desired for your finished card. Oil the back so that the design becomes transparent and is more readily seen. Designs containing lettering must *always* be pasted facedown, otherwise they would read backward in the print.

A variety of papers is available for greeting cards; Japanese and Chinese papers are especially beautiful. Bogus paper commonly called "screenings" is quite suitable for this type of work.[1] Avoid glossy papers; they do not take the ink so well as soft, absorbent kinds. Many more and attractive effects may be worked out by using combinations of materials. These uses of block printing permit free sway to the creative faculty, thus proving that wood engraving is more than a reproductive art.

The print may be made on any of the papers suggested and "tipped" or pasted onto a mount of heavier stock of a different color. Another idea is to fasten the print inside a little folder, as is done on so many conventional Christmas cards. Do not fail to consider the possibilities that lie in the use of colored inks on different colored papers. For printing greeting cards, bookplates, labels, etc. the wringer will be found most useful. A cardboard kit, to which the block can be glued, will prevent slipping. Such a kit is discussed elsewhere in this book, namely on page 17 of Chapter II.

Sometimes suitable letter paper or correspondence cards may be purchased and the linoleum block cut to fit them.[2] This is a good idea to consider when only a small edition of cards is to be issued.

Gold and silver printing inks are for sale, but a very simple way to print your motif in metallic colors is to print the

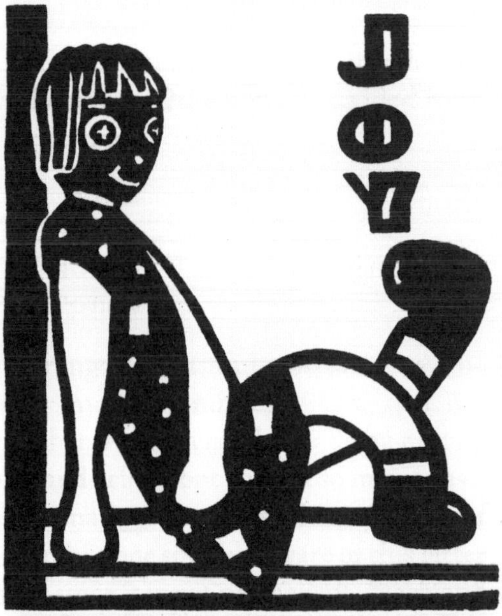

Xmas Menu Card—Student

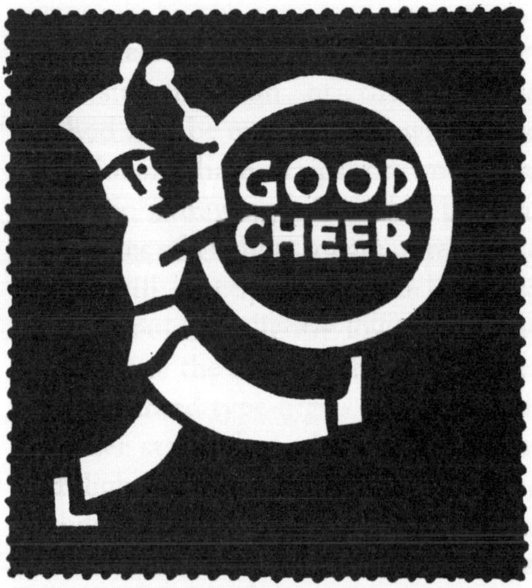

Xmas Card—E. Ottoson

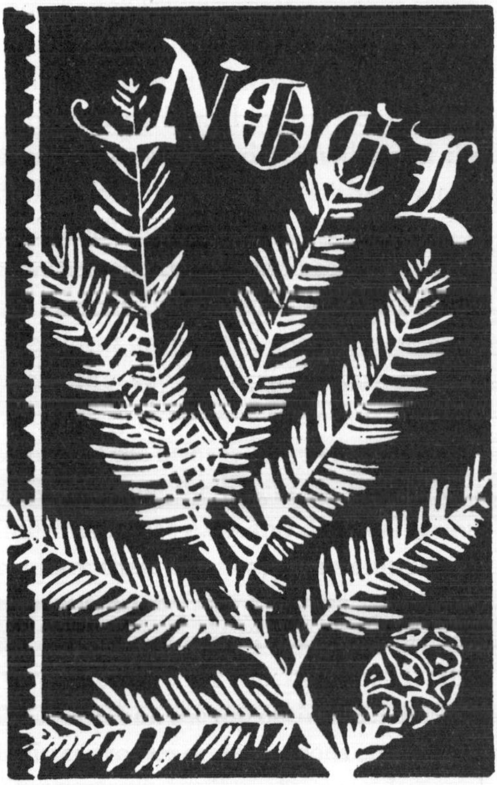

Xmas Card

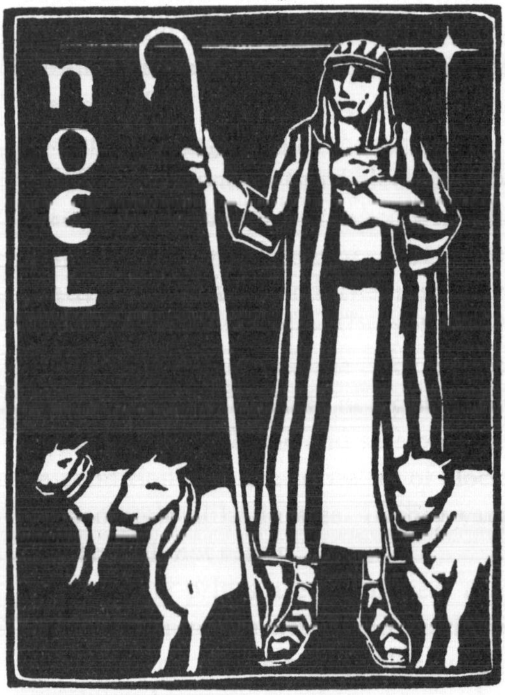

Xmas Card—F. Corson

design with regular printing ink, yellow for example, and with a soft, dry brush dust powdered gold over the prints while the ink is still wet. When dry, rub the loose powder off by means of a soft, dry brush or a wad of cotton.

Bookplates are labels pasted in books to denote their ownership. The phrase "Ex Libris – John Blake" denotes to the borrower that the book is from the collection or library of John Blake. A decorative motif, the owner's coat of arms, or a symbol suggesting some hobby of the owner may be used on the bookplate. Suitable sizes for bookplates are 1½ by 2½ inch and 2 by 3 inch.

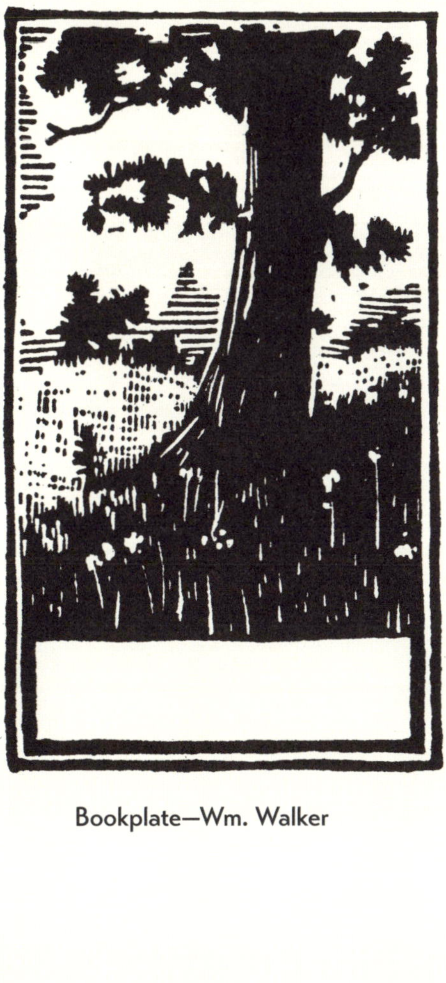

Bookplate—Wm. Walker

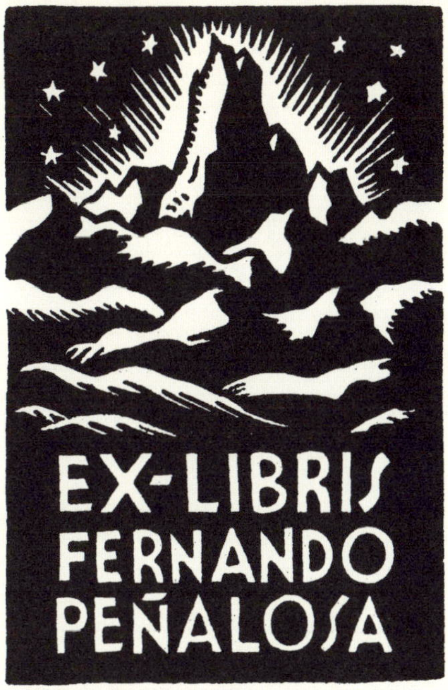

Bookplate

A linoleum block–cut bookplate is a welcome gift to anyone who owns a library, since with the block once cut, the recipient may have any number of proofs struck off on a commercial printing press. Blocks should be mounted type-high in this case.

Christmas seals for letters, tags to be attached to gifts, and menu-card covers may be made by means of block prints. One may cut tags out of stiff cover stock, make a hole with a card punch, and attach a red cord. The designs may be brightened by touching in by hand with a small brush bright show card colors or gold or silver paint. This latter method is not regarded as a strictly block-print method but rather as a compromise or mixture of methods permissible in this instance.

NOTES

1 "Screenings" were byproducts of papermaking crafted from cellulose waste screened out of the wood pulp during the refining process.

2 Correspondence cards are a type of stationery suited to brief letters. They are unembellished, of heavier cardstock, and of more general use than standard thank-you, greeting, or note cards.

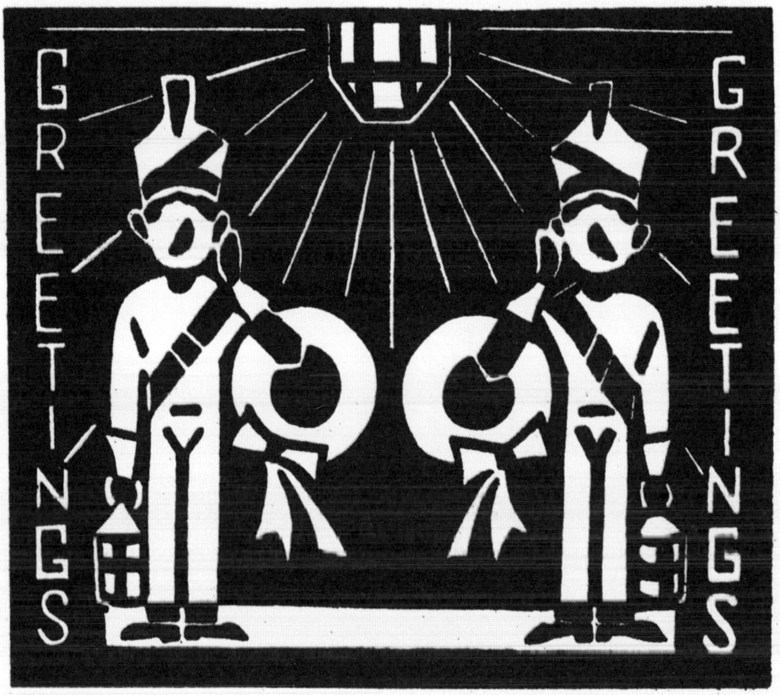

Xmas Menu Card—M. Marlais

CHAPTER XIII

APPLICATION OF BLOCK PRINTING TO ARTICLES OF USE OR BEAUTY

Block printing is more than an artistic pastime, for it has many practical uses. In commercial art, block printing lends itself quite readily, especially when its possibilities and limitations are fully understood. Advertising undoubtedly offers the widest field for use of block printing. This is especially true when business concerns find that they can use the same design in a variety of colors, even though the run may not be large. The low cost of production in block printing is an added inducement to the businessman. Hence the block print is an ideal medium for this kind of advertising art.

The poster, too, in its various forms such as car, window, and counter cards, furnishes ample opportunities for using the block print at a reasonable cost. The "snappy" lines and broad masses of block prints naturally lend themselves to poster design. Since a poster is usually seen at a considerable distance – often, too, on the run – the story must be told directly and forcibly so that it may be understood at a glance. The businessman who wishes to keep his product before the eyes of the public cannot fail to take advantage of its possibilities.

In addition to posters, block printing can be applied to the following things used for advertising and for home and school decoration:

- Announcements
- Bookplate covers
- Bookplates
- Box covering, paper
- Cards for all occasions and purposes
- Christmas wrapping papers
- Cookie-can decorations
- Decorated print portfolio
- Doily and tablecloth decorations
- Gift labels
- Handkerchiefs
- Illuminated mottoes
- Letterheads
- Parchment lamp shades
- Party invitations
- Prints for framing
- Programs
- Stationery and handkerchief monograms
- Table runners
- Valentines
- Wall hangings

To decorate a coffee or cookie can, use this procedure: With enamel paint of any desired color, give the can a coat or two. Let it dry thoroughly, then choose a harmonizing colored paper. By means

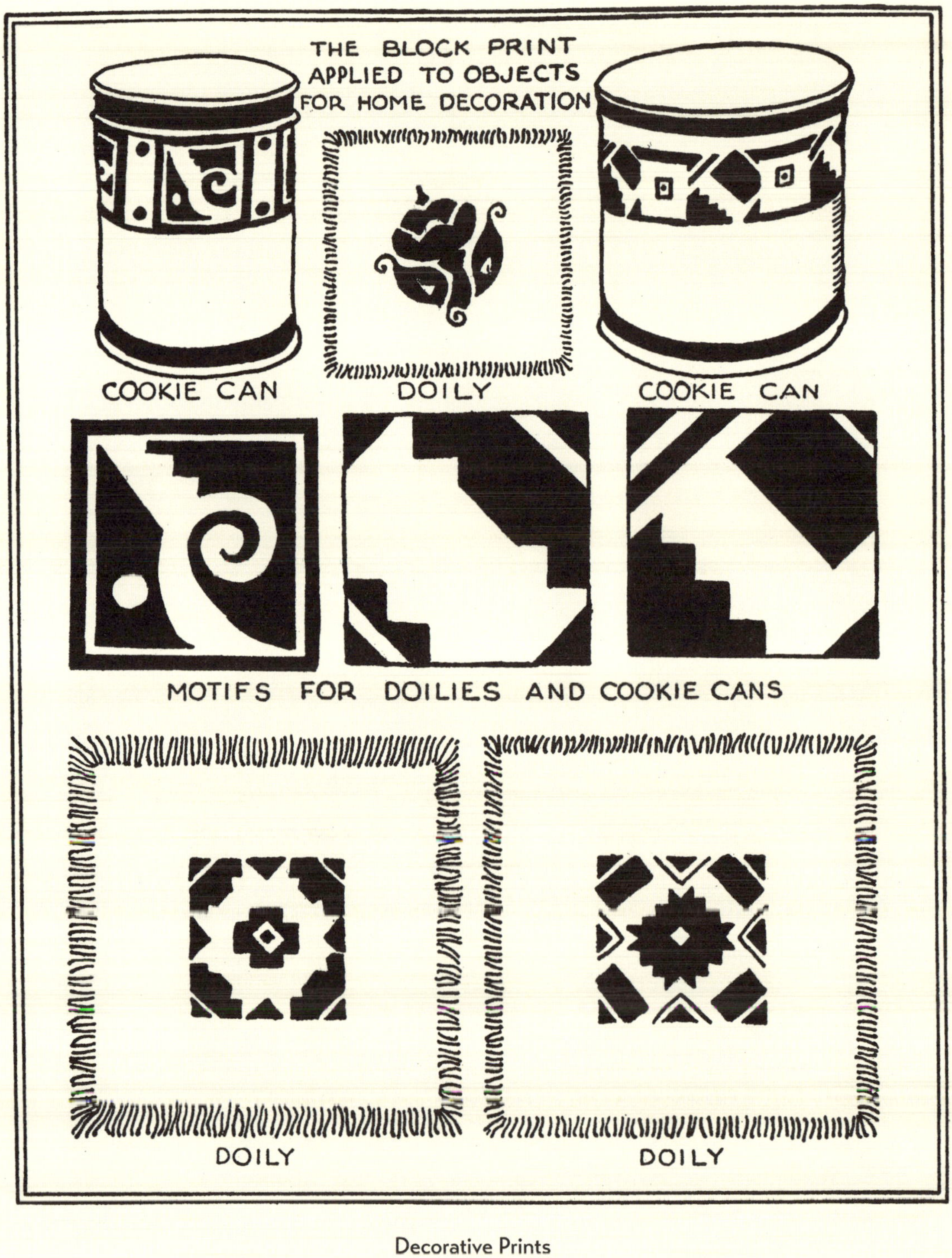

Decorative Prints

of hammer or mallet, print a small decorative design, abstract in character, on a strip of this paper cut long enough to go entirely around the can. When the print is dry, glue the paper in place and follow up with shellac or varnish.

Oilcloth table mats may be very effectively block printed in some dark color as blue, gray, or brown, and the light spaces touched in by hand with oil colors or colored inks. A small sable brush will do the work nicely.

A clever way to print Christmas wrapping paper and paper lining for booklets or portfolios is to use marbleized patterns. While this method of printing does away entirely with cut linoleum blocks, it is, nevertheless, of considerable interest to the block printer and is right in line with his work. Hence an explanation of it will be given here.

The procedure is as follows: Any kind of thin wrapping paper may be used with good results. Several oil colors or colored printing inks (oil) are thinned with kerosene in separate containers. These diluted colors are poured one after the other, into a shallow tray filled with water, and stirred about with a stick or brush, using a circular motion. The paper is then picked up by its opposite corners and carefully laid on the water surface. It picks up the pattern almost immediately. Three or four prints may be made before the colors have to be renewed.

Leather or velvet bookends decorated with block-printed designs are very artistic and effective. The key block only should be printed on the fabric and bright, contrasting colors may afterward be painted by hand.

To the enthusiastic block printer, many new ideas will suggest themselves as he continues working with this absorbing medium.

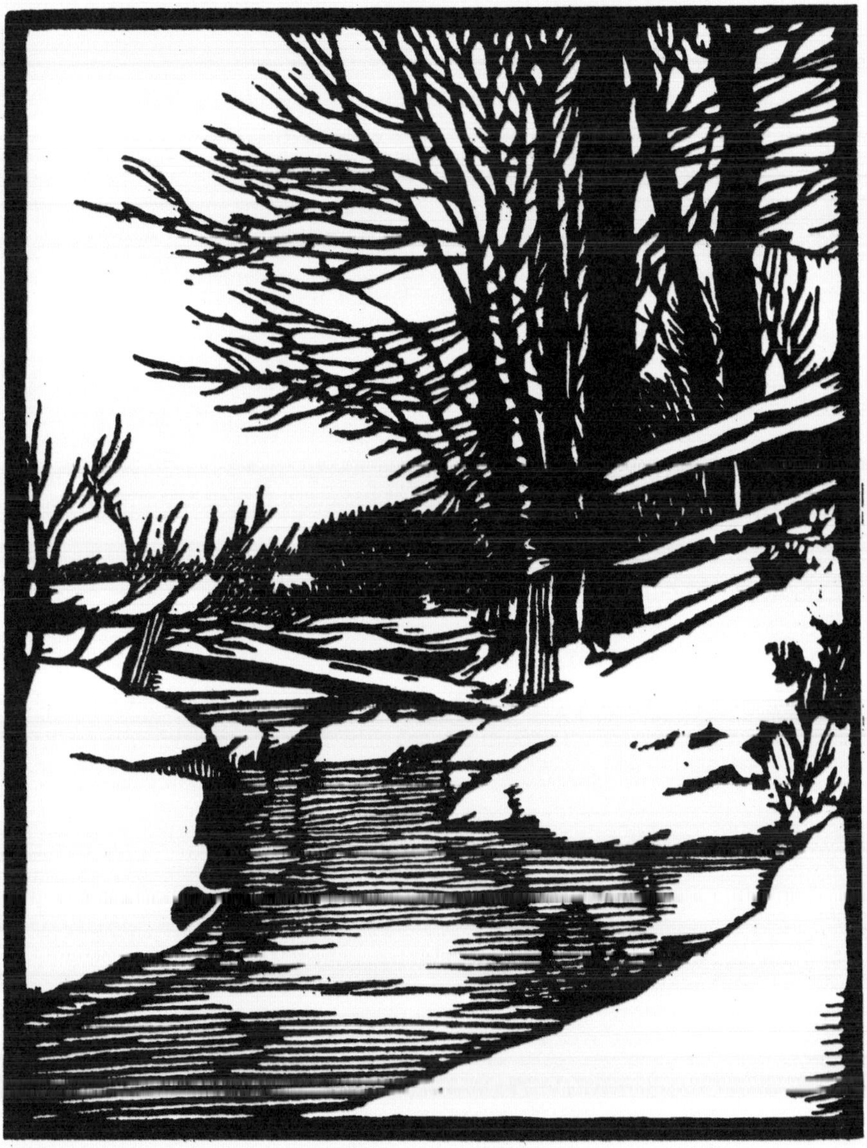

Winter in Pennsylvania

GLOSSARY

ART PRINCIPLES. Composition, design, harmony, balance, spacing, rhythm, dark and light, perspective, etc.

BAREN. A porcelain, wood, or bamboo leaf–covered tool for rubbing on the back of the paper to obtain a print or impression from the inked block.

BENCH HOOK. A wooden device to keep the block from skidding while being carved.

BLOCK. A block of engraved or carved wood or linoleum from which to make a print.

BLOCK PRINTING. A general term used for printing from wood, linoleum, rubber, or composition blocks.

BRAYER. A roller used to ink the block.

BRISTOL BOARD. Heavy paper used for making mats for prints.

BRUSHES. Flat (No. 3) sables (½ inch), and round for applying color to blocks.

BURNISHER. Same as baren.

CARBORUNDUM WHEEL AND STONES. Stones used for grinding and sharpening cutting tools.

CHIAROSCURO METHOD. A method of making prints in monochrome from two or more blocks (usually two), one for the outline and the other for a tint or halftone; a method popular in the earlier sixteenth century in Italy and Germany.

COLOR BLOCK PRINT. A print in color made from a series of relief blocks.

COMPOSITION. Organized design; arrangement.

DABBER. A leather-covered pad used by some printers instead of a brayer or roller to ink the engraved block.

EDITION. The entire number (100 more or less) of prints made of a single subject.

ETCHING PRESS. A metal press based on the principle of a clothes wringer but capable of considerably more pressure; used to print etchings, drypoints, and sometimes linoleum blocks.

GOUGE. A cutting tool with a curved blade used to remove the larger areas of a block. They are U and V shaped.

GRADATION IN PRINTING. A process of printing from a single block a graded or blended tone ranging from dark to light.

INK ROLLER. Professionally called a "brayer."

INKS (PRINTING). Inks which come in tubes and which have either an oil or water base.

JAPANESE HOSHO PAPER. Very absorbent paper with a high-grade texture.

JIGGER. A heavy pasteboard-hinged mat to hold the cut and paper in place without slipping during the printing process; used with either a wringer or etching press.

KEY BLOCK. The block containing the main design in dark and light outlines and masses.

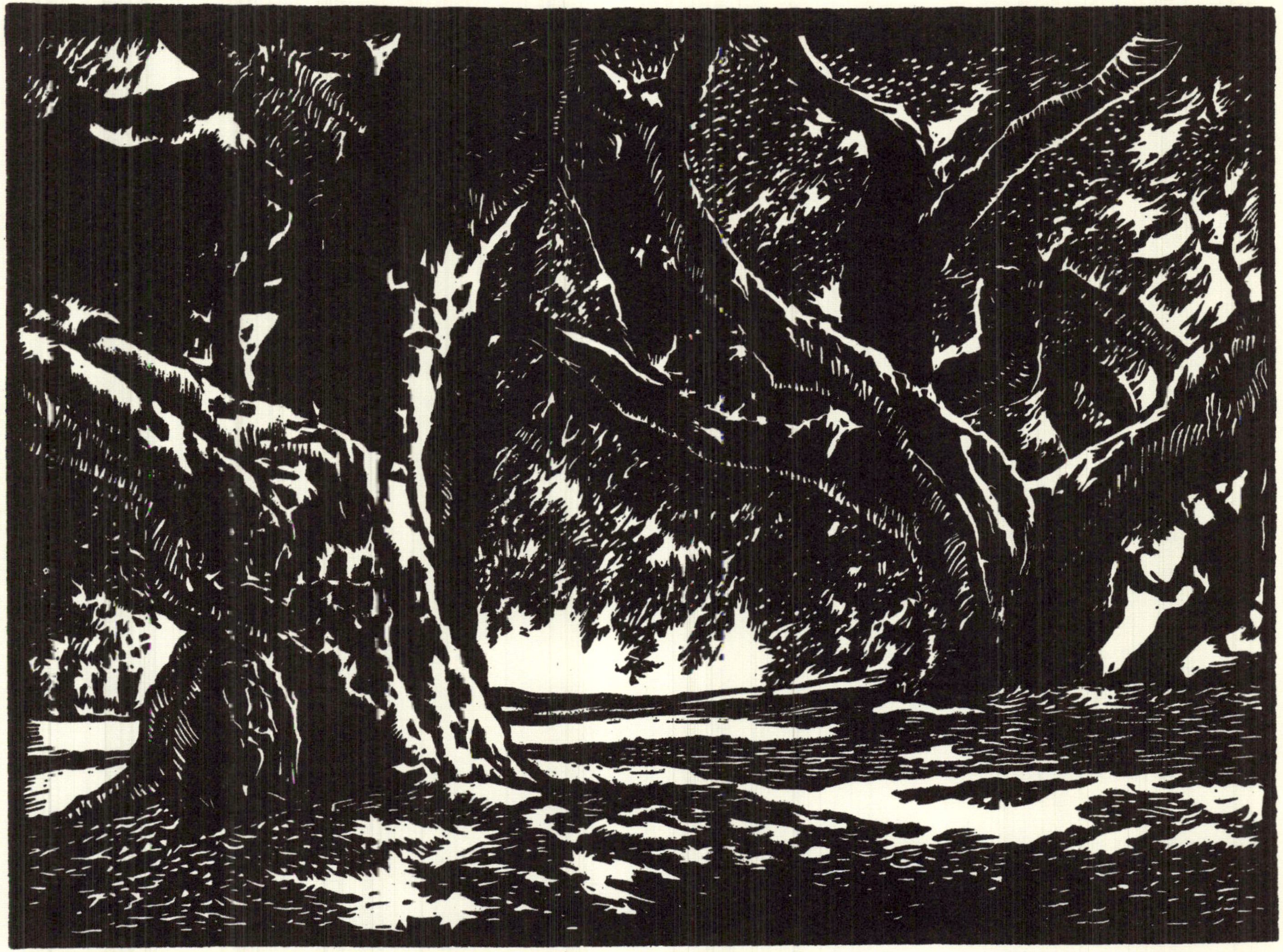

Forest Primeval

LETTERPRESS. An old-fashioned press used formerly for duplicating letters, now very useful for block printing.

LINOLEUM (BLOCKS). A material excellent for block cutting because of its lack of grain. Battleship, unpatterned is best.

MATS. Cardboard mounts to protect prints when handling or exhibiting.

MULTIPLE BLOCKS. More than one block; term used in color printing.

OFFSET PRINT. A method of transferring the design to other blocks intended for printing color, by making a proof and laying it, while wet, facedown on clean blocks and rubbing it on the back with a spoon or baren.

PALETTE KNIFE. A flexible knife used by artists to mix colors on the palette or inks on the color slab.

PHOTO REPRODUCTION. Photoengraving or mechanical engraving.

PLATEN (PLATE). A heavy metal casting on a letterpress, the lower surface of which is flat and smooth.

POSTER PAINT. Opaque watercolors used for painting posters, etc.

PRINTING FRAME. A wooden frame similar in principle to a press and used for proofing.

PROOF. A trial print.

QUOINS. Wedges to lock the block in a printing frame.

REGISTER. A term used in color printing meaning to adjust one color block with the print of another so that the color impressions will fit in their correct relationship on the finished print.

REVERSED PROOF. A proof taken by pressing a sheet of dampened paper against a wet proof; to be used as a guide for making alterations or color notations.

RIPPLE-FINISH PAPER. Paper of uneven surface used for mats.

ROUTING. A term used by engravers meaning to clear out backgrounds.

SILHOUETTES. Flat profiles, white or black, of human heads, animals, trees, or flowers, etc.

SLIPSTONES. Thin, wedge-shaped stones used to sharpen gouges.

"TIF TOOLS" (SPEEDBALL CUTTERS). Cutting tools with blades of different sizes and shapes which may be inserted in handles somewhat like penholders.

TONAL PAPER. Inexpensive construction papers in various colors, tints, and shades; very useful for experimental printing.

TYPE-HIGH. The height of type; necessary height of a block to be printed with a commercial printing press; usually .9186 inch.

VEINING TOOL. A small V-shaped gouge used for outlining a design on the block.

WOOD. Used in woodcuts; boxwood, apple, pear, red gum, basswood, and sugar pine. Wood is more difficult to cut than linoleum because of grain.

WOODCUT. A wood engraving cut or gouged with the grain of the wood.

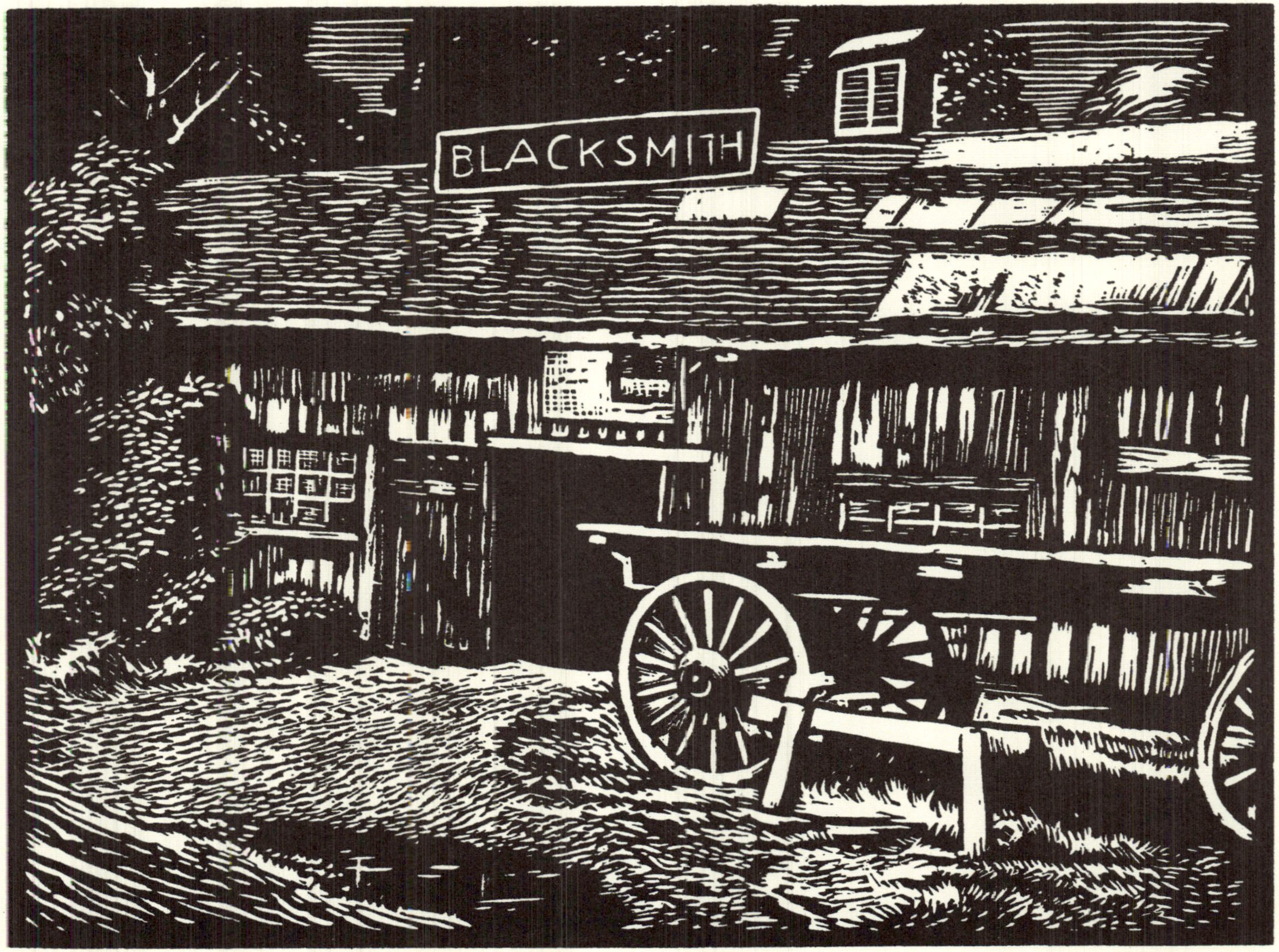

Old Blacksmith Shop—California

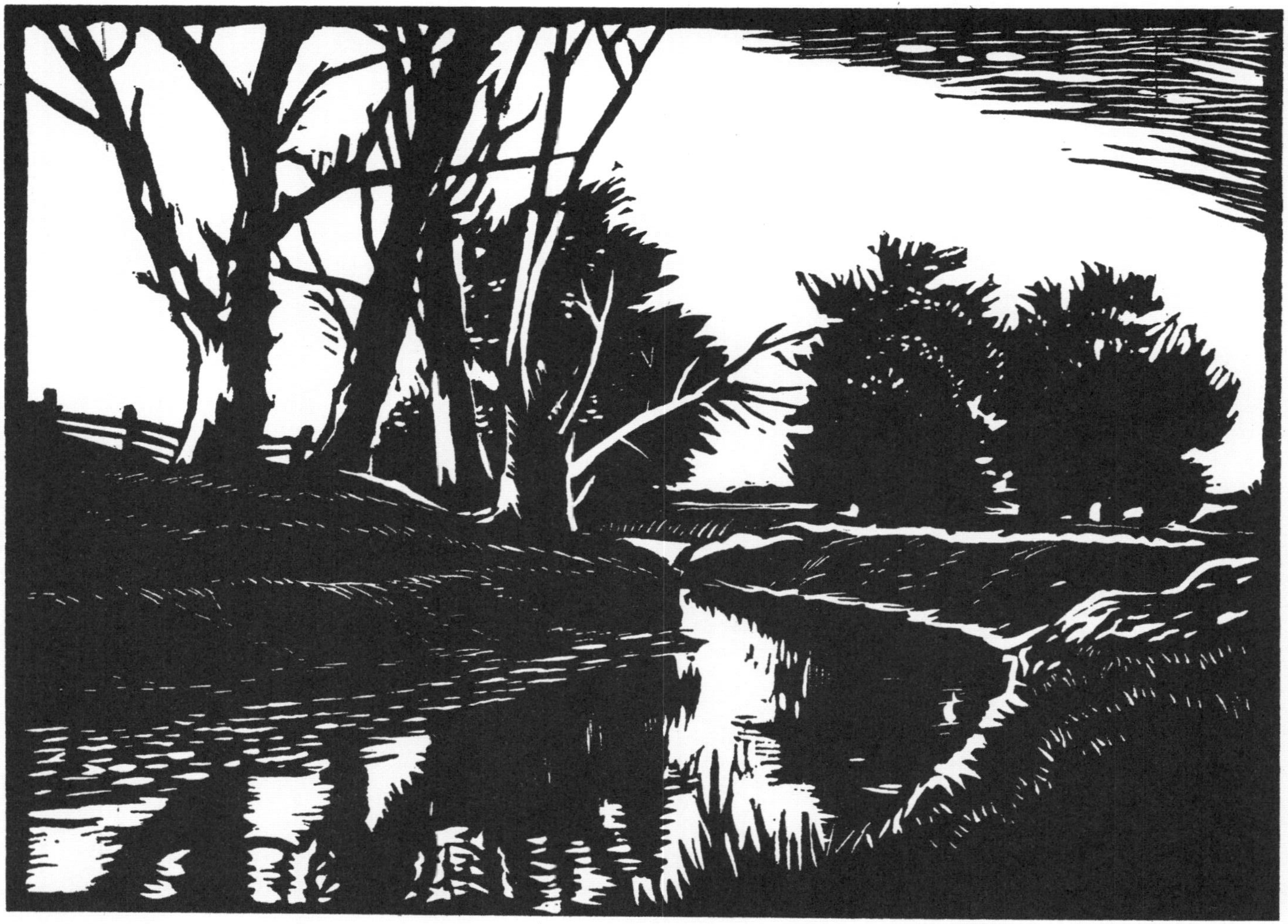

Reiff's Run

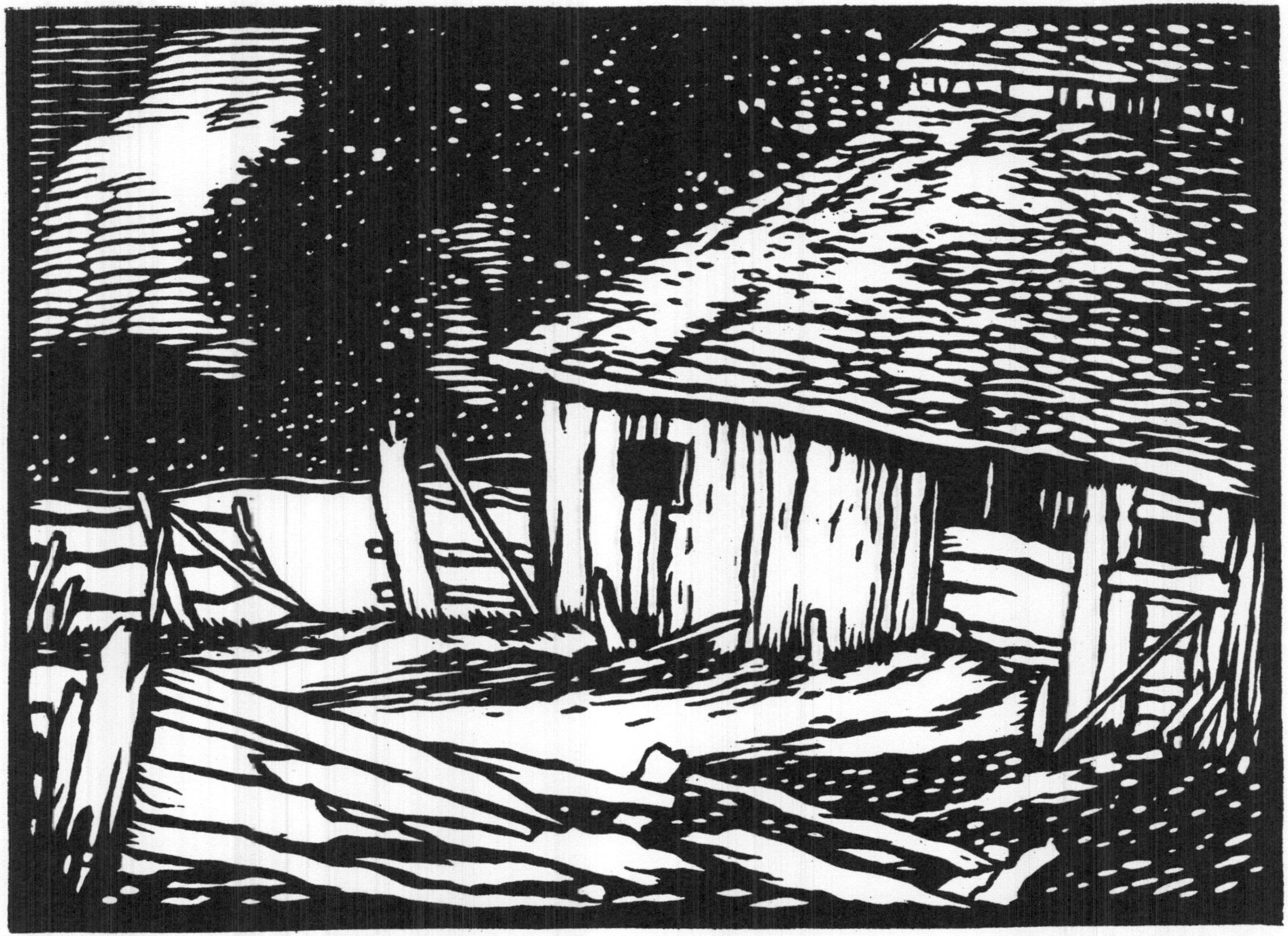

Deserted Barn—Wm. Fitch

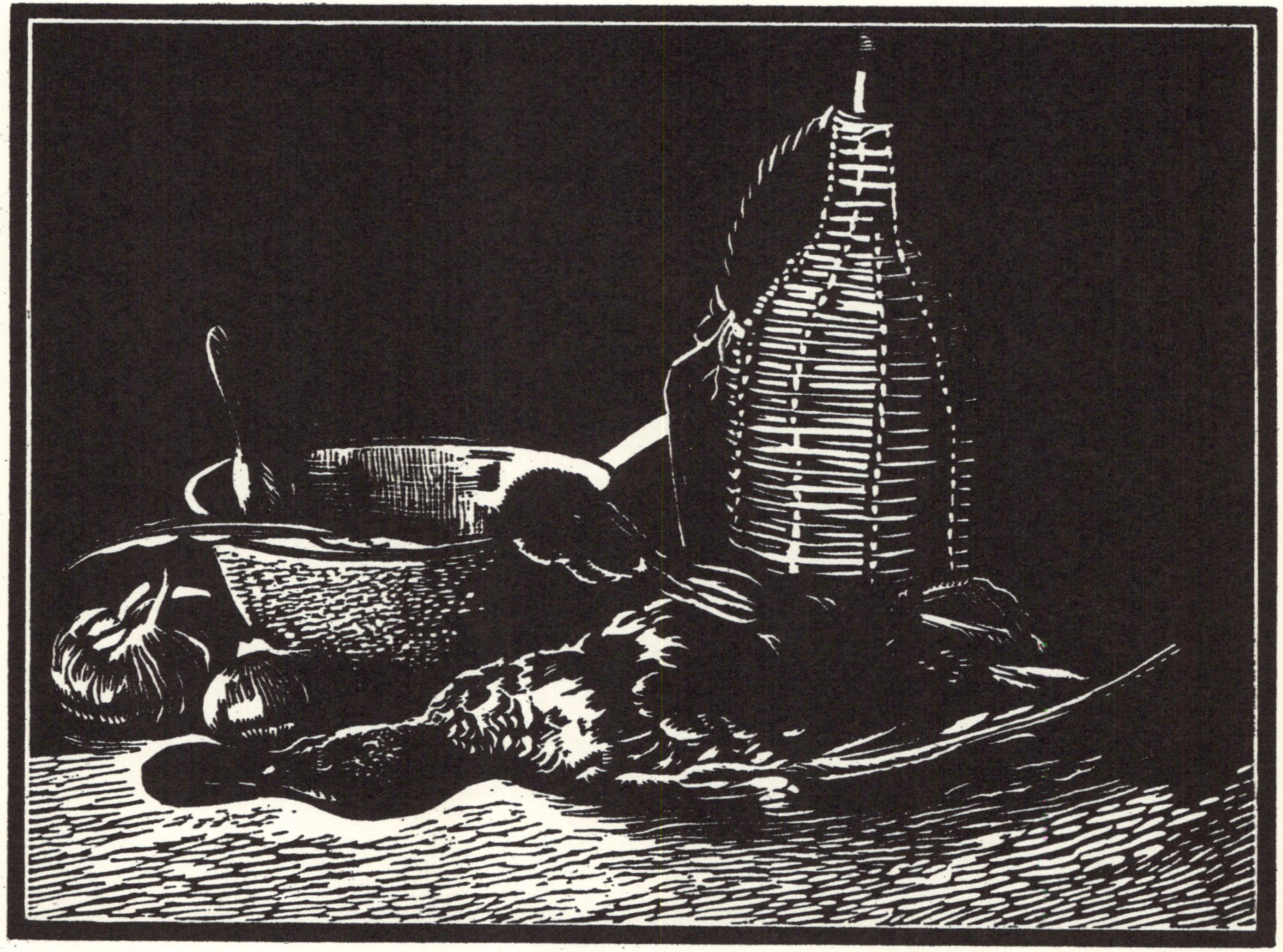

Ducks for Dinner

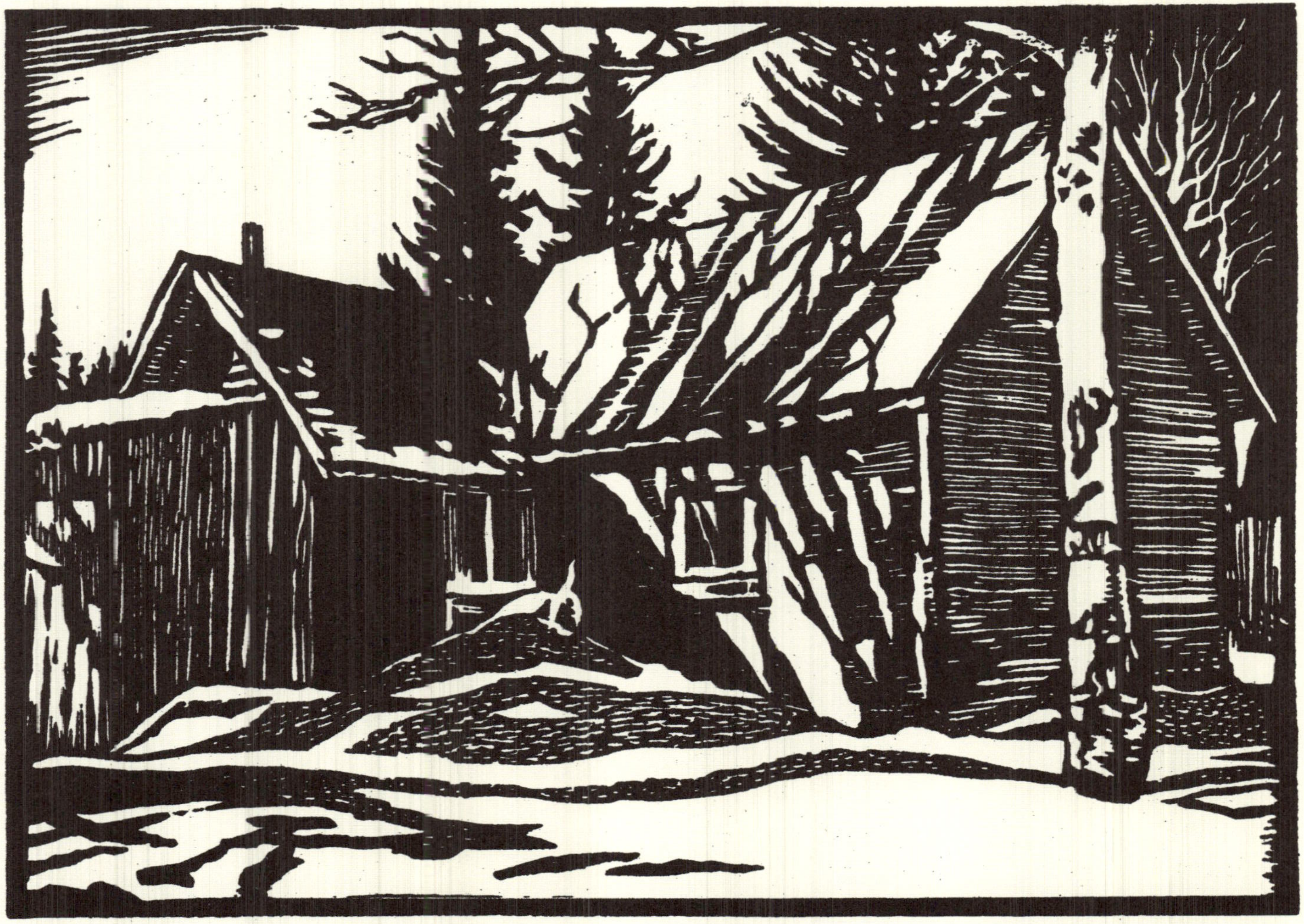

Trapper's Cabin—Vermont

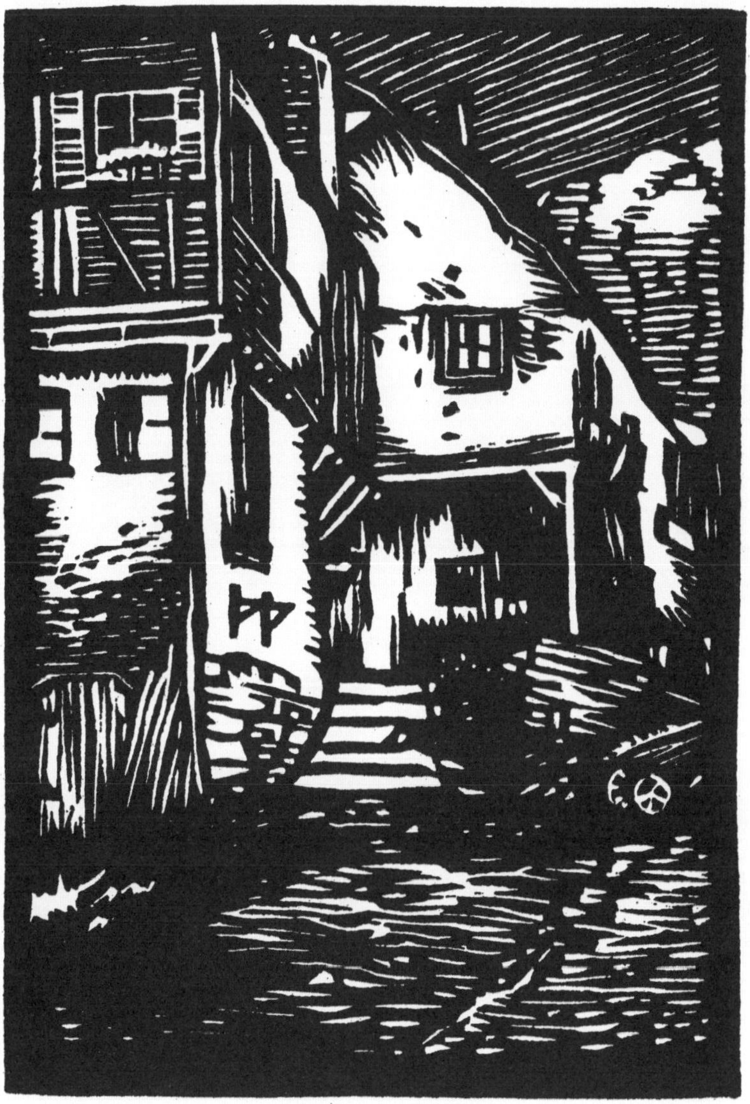

Old Houses—Wm. Fitch

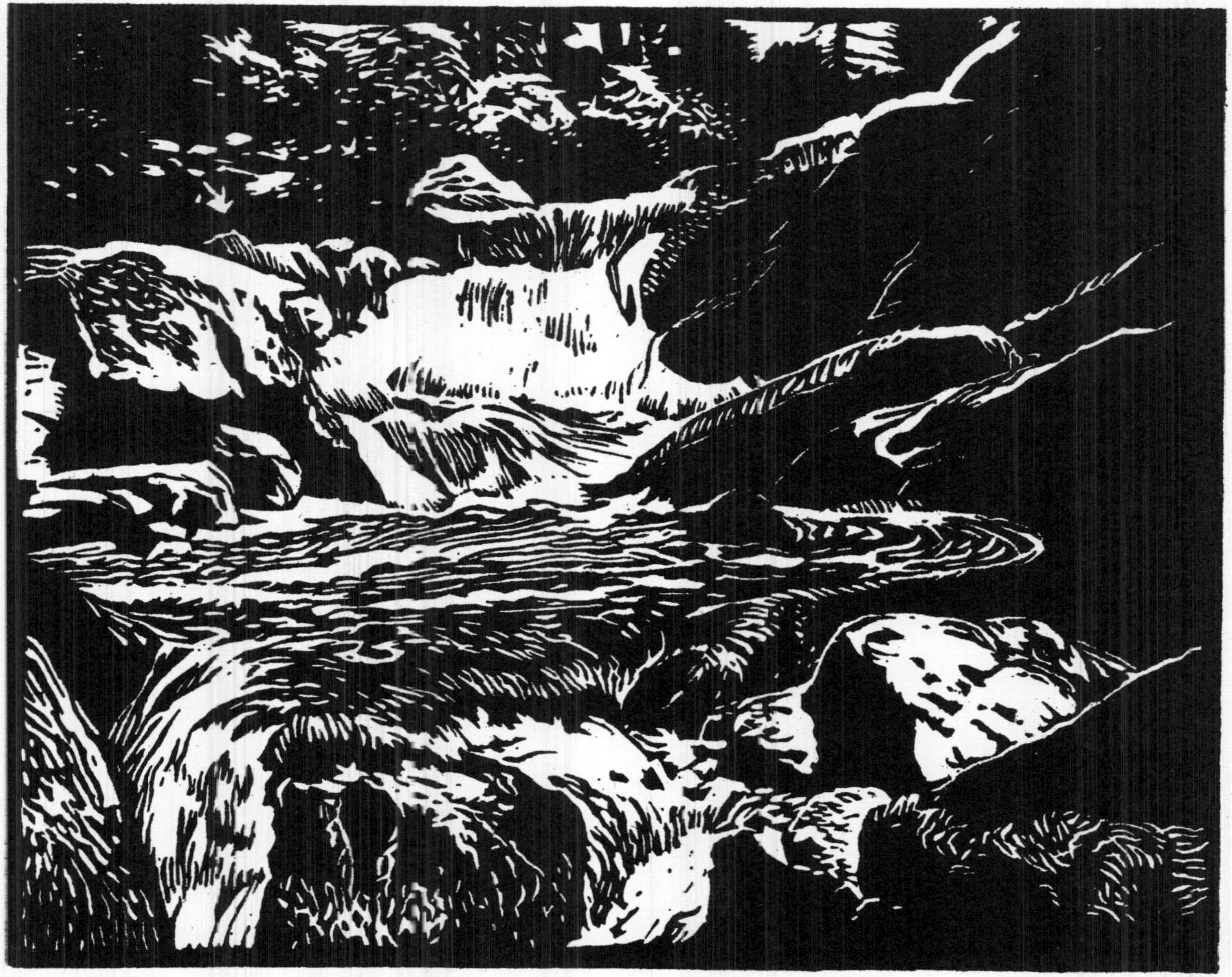

Cascade-Yosemite Valley

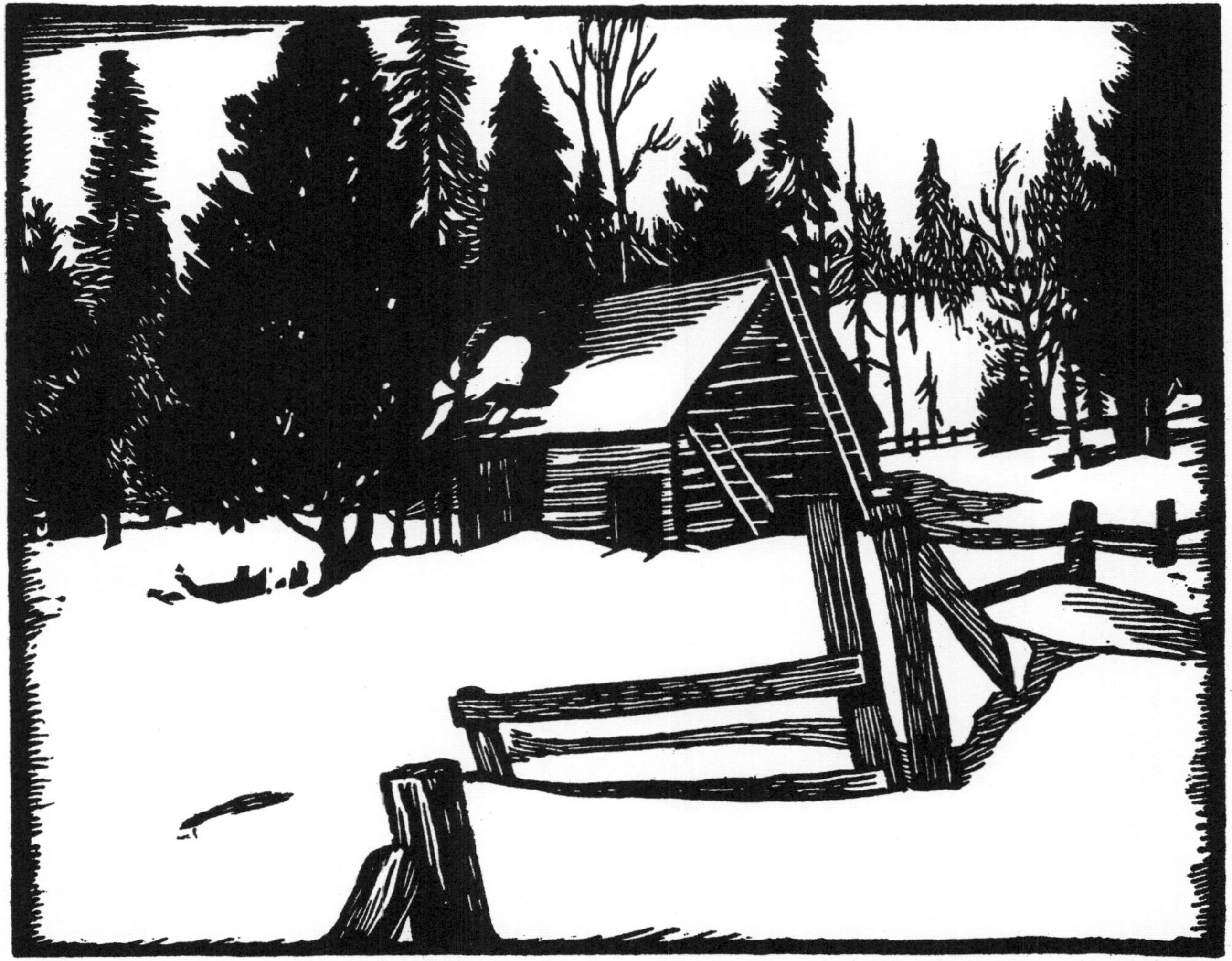

Barn in Calaveras

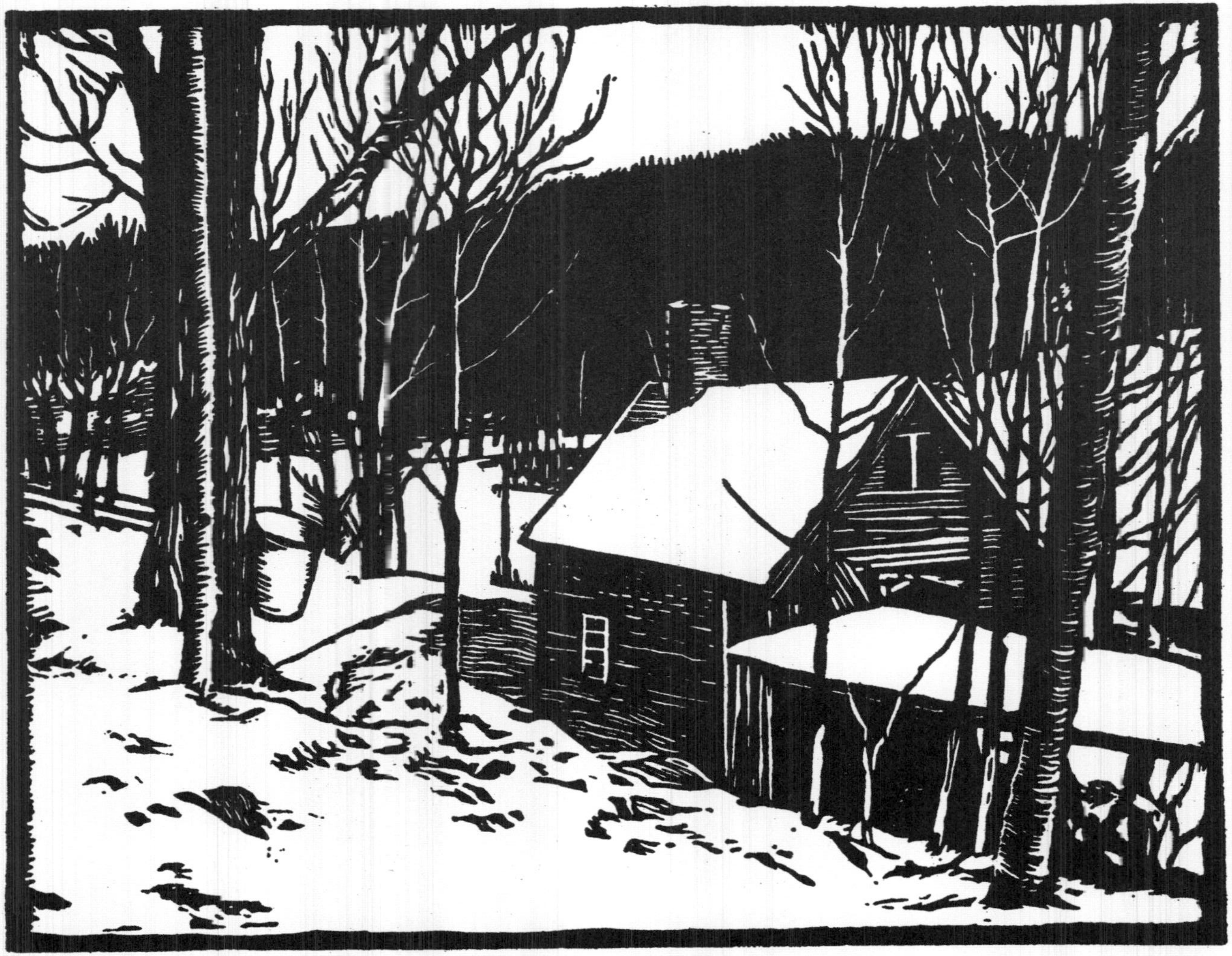

Maple Sugar Camp—Vermont

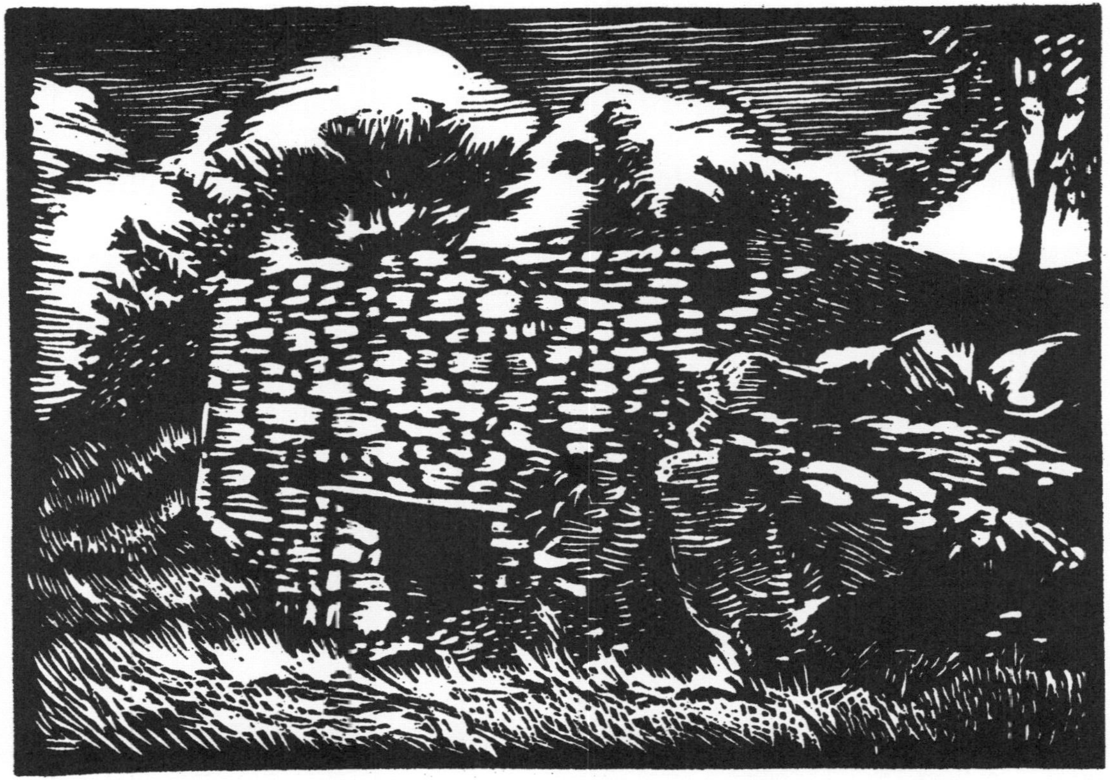

Old Limekiln

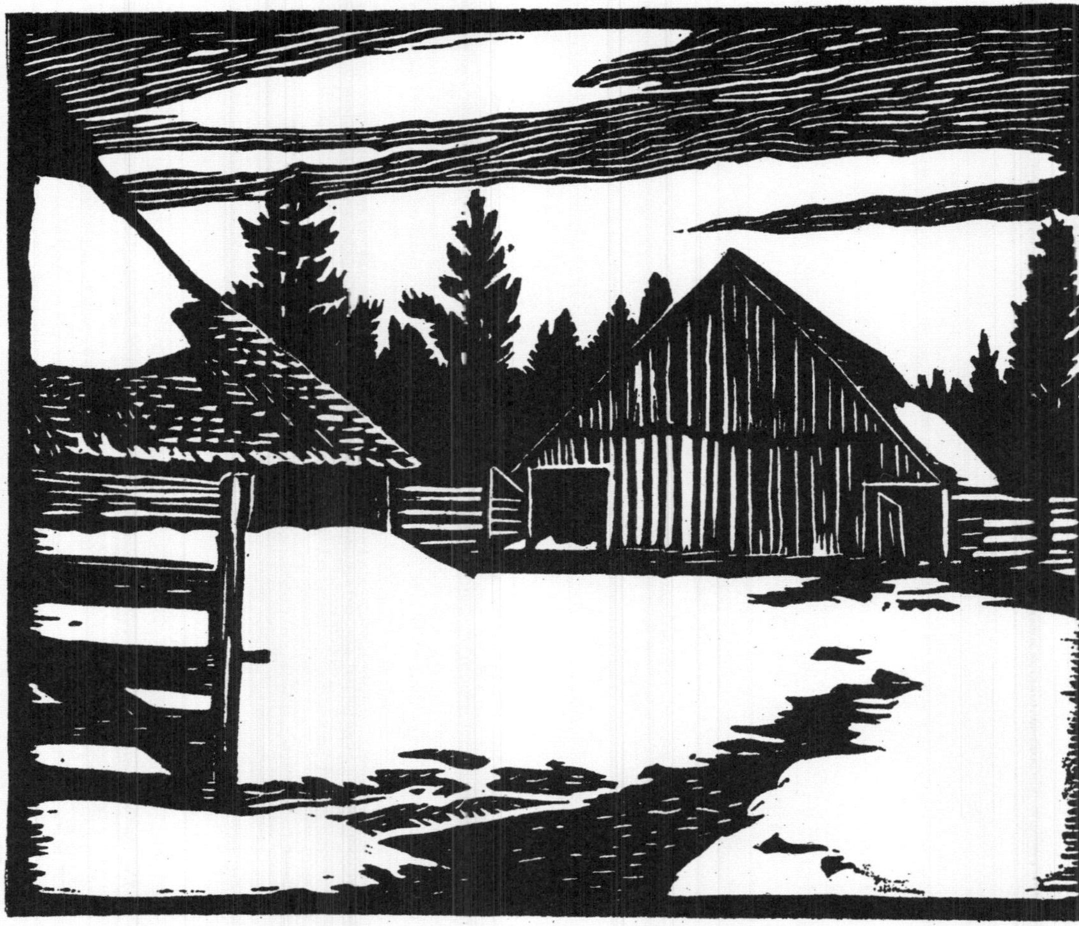

Sierra Barns

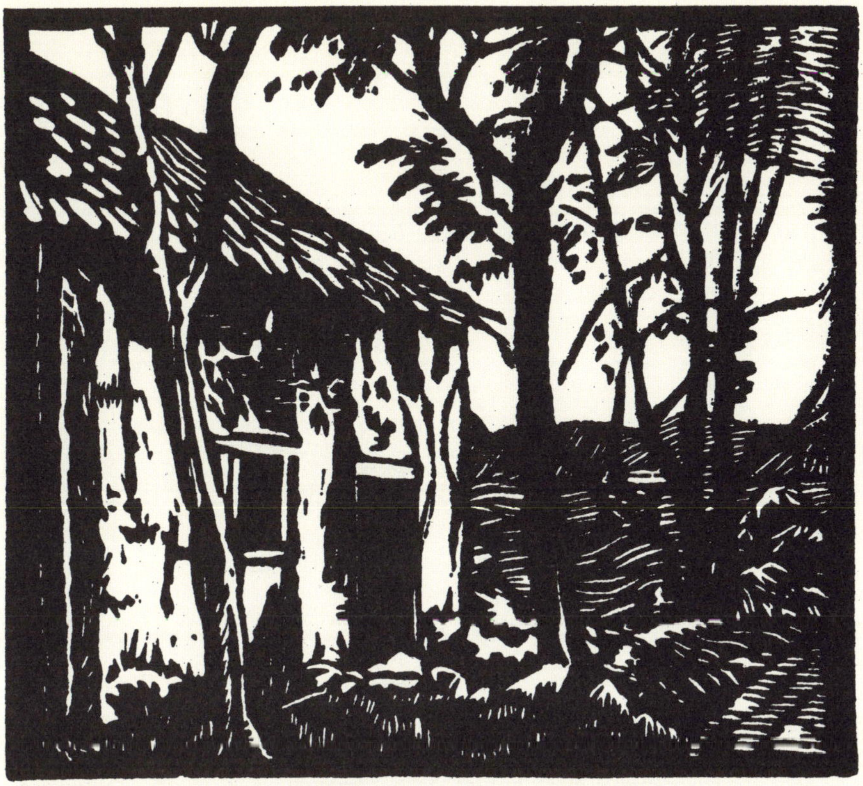

Old Adobe—Mokelumne Hill

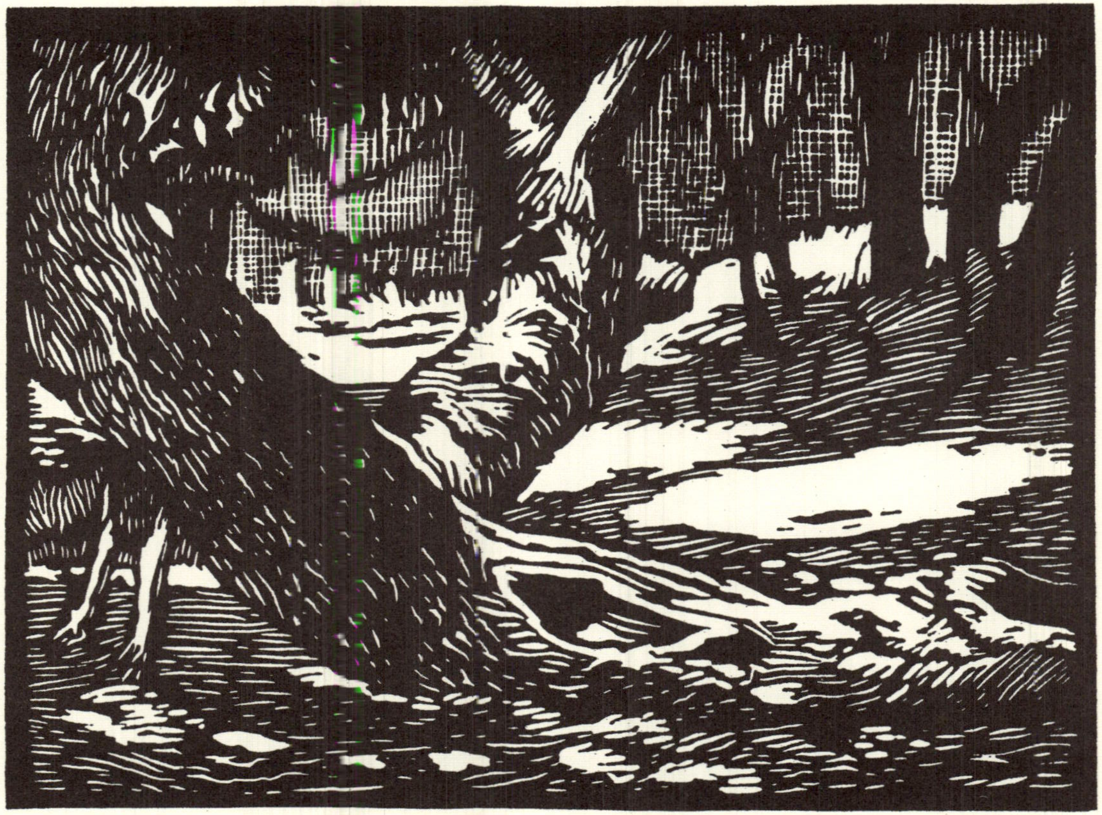

Western Sycamores

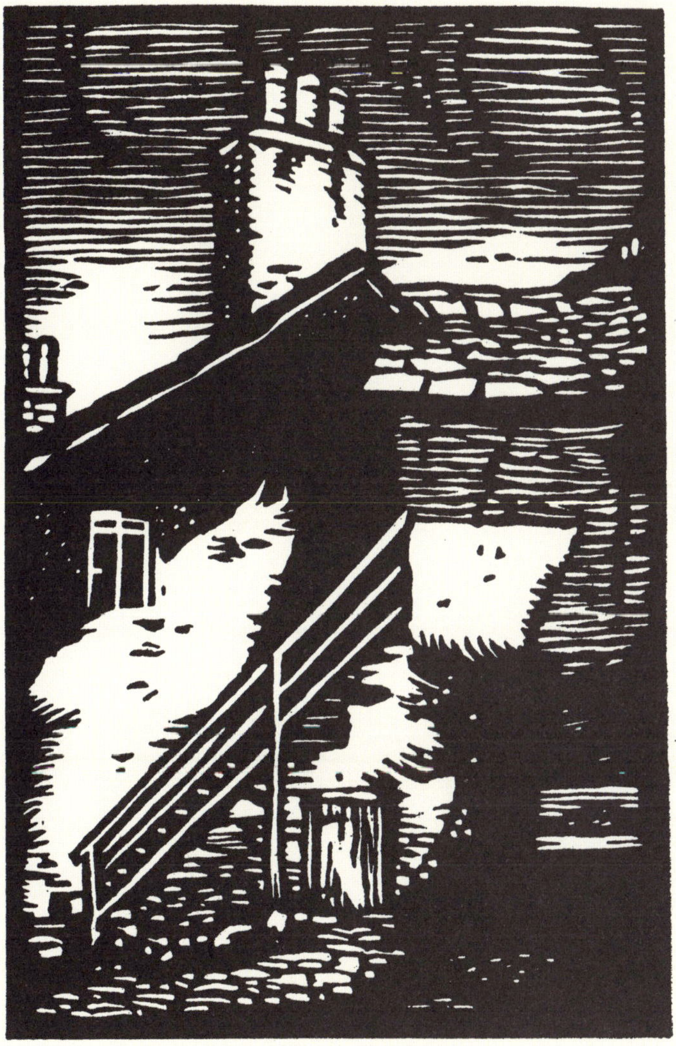

Back Yards—Wm. Fitch

ABOUT THE AUTHORS

At the time of this book's original publication, in 1941, **William Seltzer Rice**, BFA, gave his credentials, on the title page, as, "Instructor, University of California Extension Department, and formerly instructor in block printing, California College of Arts and Crafts, Oakland, California." For more biographical information, see Martin Krause's introduction to this edition.

Martin Krause served for thirty-nine years as curator of prints, drawings, and photographs at the Indianapolis Museum of Art at Newfields. Krause is coauthor of *Gustave Baumann: Nearer to Art* and editor of *The Autobiography of Gustave Baumann* (Pomegranate, 2015) and *Gustave Baumann: Views of Brown County* (Pomegranate, 2018). His other wide-ranging publications devoted to the history of the graphic arts include monographs on J. M. W. Turner, Robert Indiana, and Garo Antreasian.